# Successful Resumes and Interviews

Carl Perrin
*Casco Bay College, Portland, Maine*

Peter Dublin
*Intentional Educations, Watertown, Mass.*

Delmar Publishers Inc.™

I(T)P™

# NOTICE TO THE READER

**Cover photo by Joe Mulone/The Photographers & Co.**

Delmar Staff:

Senior Acquisitions Editor: Mary McGarry
Project Editor: Theresa M. Bobear
Production Coordinator: James Zayicek
Art & Design Cooardinator: Karen Kunz Kemp

For information, address Delmar Publishers Inc.
3 Columbia Circle, Box 15-015,
Albany, NY 12212-5015

© Copyright 1994 by Delmar Publishers Inc.
The trademark ITP is used under license.

**Delmar Publishers' Online Services**
To access Delmar on the World Wide Web, point your browser to:
**http://www.delmar.com/delmar.html**
To access through Gopher: gopher://gopher.delmar.com
(Delmar Online is part of "thomson.com", an Internet site with information on more than 30 publishers of the International Thomson Publishing organization.)
For information on our products and services:
email: info@delmar.com
or call 800-347-7707

Printed in the United States of America
Published simultaneously in Canada
by Nelson Canada,
a division of The Thomson Corporation

2   3   4   5   6   7   8   9   10      XXX      00   99   98   97   96

**Library of Congress Cataloging-in-Publication Data**

Perrin, Carl.
    Successful resumes and interviews  / Carl Perrin, Peter Dublin.
        p.   cm.
    Includes index.
    ISBN 0-8273-5991-8
    1. Résumés (Employment)   2. Employment interviewing.   I. Dublin,
Peter.  II. Title.
HF5383.P428   1994
650.14—dc20

93-4925
CIP

# Table of Contents

# Preface

For the past fifteen years, I have taught at Casco Bay College, a small, two-year business college in Portland, Maine. During this period, virtually all of our graduates have found jobs in their respective fields. We believe that part of the reason for this highly successful job placement rate is our Interview Seminar in which we teach our students how to prepare resumes and cover letters, advise them about using our college job placement service, and let them know what to expect in interviews.

I have been associated with the Interview Seminar since I began at Casco Bay College and have directed the program for the past eight years. During this time, I have learned much that can be valuable to job seekers. I have written *Successful Resumes and Interviews* to share some of this knowledge with readers who will be entering the job market for the first time or who are interested in reentering the job market to find better positions.

The students in our evening program at the college are primarily people who are already working in business and are seeking to upgrade their skills to get better jobs. I have learned that even individuals who have been in the business world for some time are often perplexed when facing the task of preparing their resumes. I have known of people, for example, who have written seven- and ten-page resumes. Some students know that resumes should not be more than two pages but are unsure of what to omit and still include college and part-time work experience. This book will help readers to both write more effective, concise, and confident resumes and prepare for job interviews.

I also found that people have almost as much trouble preparing a cover letter as they do with their resumes. Whereas they often make their resumes too long, they tend to make their cover letters too short and insubstantial. They view their cover letters as little more than a transmittal letter. Cover letters can enhance a resume, individualize a job application, relate a person's qualifications to the specific positions they seek, and make them more attractive as job candidates.

To provide you with the guidance and help that you may need in getting the job you want, this book is divided into seven chapters and two appendices. Chapter 1, "Preparing to Write Your Resume," helps you learn the requirements of a job and prepare an inventory of your qualifications. Chapter 2, "Writing a Successful Resume," discusses the characteristics of an effective resume, explains what ought and ought not go into your resume, and focuses on the format and length of a successful resume. Chapter 3, "Using Hypothetical Cases to Find Your Format," illustrates five different formats for writing your resume by following five different characters through varied work-related situations and levels of experience. Chapter 4, "Developing an Effective Cover Letter," covers the four types of cover letters and provides information to help you write your own effective cover letter.

In Chapter 5, "Preparing for Your Interview," we move from the resume to the job interview, discuss the purpose of the job interview, focus on developing a positive attitude prior to your interview, explain what the interviewer is looking for, and cover final preparations for your interview. In Chapter 6, "Making a Good Impression During Your Interview," we focus on your arrival for an interview, the types of interviewers and interviews that you may encounter, the questions frequently asked in an interview, what your interviewer may and may not ask you, and deal with rejection if you don't get the job you wanted. Finally, in Chapter 7, "Writing a Good Follow-Up Letter," we take the job hunting process to its conclusion and discuss the thank-you letter, the follow-up letter, and the I-didn't-get-the-job-but-thanks-anyway letter.

In Appendix A, 14 model resumes are provided, representing job applicants in various fields of work. These resumes can be used to find one that is similar to your career field and ambitions and might be helpful as a model as you prepare a resume of your own. In Appendix B, you will find a checklist for job seekers. This checklist will help you make the initial preparations for your job search, guide you through the creation of your own resume and cover letter, prepare you for your interview, and assist you in writing your follow-up letter.

In addition, the software disk accompanying *Successful Resumes and Interviews* contains a full-functioning word processor along with on-line lessons and activities. Also on-line, a simple database manager is provided that you can use to store relevant information regarding resume writing. The software applications, linked to Chapters 1, 2, 3, 4, and 7 and described at the end of the text, serve as a guide for using the database in developing your own resumes and cover and follow-up letters. In completing these activities, you will be applying what you have learned, reinforcing your knowledge, and developing essential writing and researching skills. You will also begin to develop files of actual resumes, cover letters, and other resources that can be valuable to you when you seek employment.

At the back of the text, you will find a Glossary of terminology that may be unfamiliar to you and a Bibliography of sources you might want to seek out if you are interested in learning more about any of the topics covered.

I extend my heartfelt gratitude to the following reviewers, whose queries, comments, and suggestions were so instrumental in creating the book that you hold in your hands:

- Carole Armstrong, Clinton Vocational Center, Clinton, MS

- Katherine Benincasa, Patchogue-Medford Central School District Junior High School, Patchogue, NY

- Ruth Buell, J. Everett Light Career Center, Indianapolis, IN

- Rose Lamorella, Albany Adult Learning Center, Albany, NY

In addition, I would like to acknowledge my students over the years for helping me to continue to learn and to grow.

Finally, I thank Mary McGarry for recognizing the need for such a book and for seeing it through the long, arduous process from proposal to publication and Bob Nirkind for his skillful guidance as we developed a manuscript that we hope will give readers everywhere the tools they need to win the jobs they seek.

Whether you are in high school or college, preparing for your first professional job, or thinking about changing jobs, this book will give you the ammunition necessary to attack the job market. Good luck!

*Carl Perrin*

# About the Authors

**Carl Perrin** has taught English at Casco Bay College in Portland, Maine since 1978 and has been head of the English Department for the past 12 years. Since beginning at Casco Bay College, Dr. Perrin has been involved in the college's Job Interview Seminar and has directed it for the past seven years.

Before coming to Casco Bay College, Dr. Perrin worked at Goodwill of Maine, where he helped handicapped workers prepare themselves for the job market and find employment.

Previously, Dr. Perrin taught English at Defiance College in Defiance, Ohio. He has also taught at the high school level in New Hampshire, Missouri, and Maine. His works of fiction and nonfiction, as well as articles on teaching methodology, have been widely published.

Dr. Perrin received his B.A. from the University of New Hampshire, M. Ed. from River College in New Hampshire, and Ph.D. from Ohio State University.

**Peter Dublin** is the President of Intentional Educations in Watertown, Massachusetts. One of the foremost developers of educational materials in the country, Intentional Educations has developed textbooks and instructional software for all levels of education.

As President of Intentional Educations, Dr. Dublin has been involved in the publication of many educational products, including a series of high school social studies texts that he coauthored, a junior high school computer literacy text, and an elementary language arts basal textbook series. In addition, he has been involved in the development of over 100 pieces of instructional software, including the avard-winning Bank Street Writer. Dr. Dublin also founded and was the first publisher of *Classroom Computer News,* one of the first magazines designed to help teachers integrate computers into their classrooms; the magazine continues to this day as *Technology and Learning.*

Prior to becoming President of Intentional Educations, Dr. Dublin taught in the New Haven, Connecticut, and New York City public schools. He also trained teachers at the Antioch Graduate Center in Cambridge, Massachusetts.

Dr. Dublin received his B.A. from Oberlin College, his M.A.T. from Harvard University, and his Ed.D. from Teachers College, Columbia University.

# CHAPTER 1

# Preparing to Write Your Resume

## OBJECTIVES

**After you have studied this chapter, you should be able to:**

- **Determine the specific requirements for a job.**
- **Read between the lines of a want ad or job notice to discover unstated or implied job requirements.**
- **Draw up an inventory of your qualifications for a job.**
- **Present evidence of your qualifications.**
- **Show how your qualifications meet each specific job requirement.**

Let's say you have sent your resume, the sheet that summarizes your qualifications for a job, to a company for which you're interested in working. What happens to that resume? If the job has been advertised, there could be several dozen other people who have also responded to the ad. Is the interviewer, the person who conducts an employment interview,—the personnel director or department head—going to interview everyone who answers the ad? Probably not.

The interviewer may decide that she has time to interview eight people. If so, she will select these eight by a process of elimination. Some of the applicants may not really be qualified for the position; their resumes will be eliminated immediately. Other applicants may have letters or resumes with typographical or spelling errors, or that reveal a poor command of language and grammar; these applications will be eliminated in a competitive situation as well.

The interviewer will be left with a pile of resumes that reflect applicants with at least minimal qualifications for the position and basic competence in English. If more applications still must be eliminated, what does the interviewer do next? Possibly, she will compare resumes and choose those people who have good **qualifications** over those who are only minimally qualified. The criteria to be considered will include more than education and experience. The interviewer is going to review each resume to look for clues to the applicant's character and personality. She may ask herself if each applicant has such personal characteristics as *reliability, creativity, initiative, leadership*, and *organizational ability*.

As the interviewer approaches the final elimination process, she will be left with a group of applicants who appear to have more than the minimum qualifications for the job. How, then, will the interviewer decide which of these qualified candidates she is going to speak with? This final decision will not be based on the content of the resume, but on its *style*—the way it presents the qualifications of the applicant—and *format*—the way it is structured.

A good resume will not get you a job for which you are not qualified. Nor will it give you an edge over someone with better qualifications than yours. It will, however, give you a definite advantage over someone with roughly the same qualifications. This chapter will show you how to measure your qualifications against a job's requirements so that you can prepare that winning resume.

## START WITH YOUR SOURCES OF INFORMATION AND THE SPECIFIC REQUIREMENTS OF THE JOB

If you want to demonstrate your qualifications for a job, you must know the **job requirements**, or list of qualifications for a particular job opening. How you go about finding those requirements depends partly on your source of information about the job. There are three main sources of job information: *advertisements*, *friends*, and *job placement agencies*.

### ADVERTISEMENTS

How can you learn what qualifications an employer requires for a job? If you have found out about the position from an advertisement, that ad will usually list the job's requirements. For example, Figure 1-1 gives five job opportunities listed in the Help Wanted section of the Sunday paper. These job descriptions pretty much show what sort of qualifications the employer is looking for in an applicant. Let's look at each description and see what it says and what it fails to say, beginning with the advertisement for an executive secretary.

#### Executive Secretary

- Excellent secretarial skills, including typing (70 wpm), shorthand (100 wpm), and thorough knowledge of Word Perfect.

- Excellent writing, communication, and organizational skills.

- Ability to handle multiple priorities and complete special assignments independently.

- Ability to work efficiently and the desire to take on new challenges.

---

### HELP WANTED

**EXECUTIVE SECRETARY** - Excellent secretarial skills, including typing (70 wpm), shorthand (100 wpm) and word processing. Excellent writing, communication and organizational skills. Ability to handle multiple priorities and complete special assignments independently. Ability to work efficiently and the desire to take on new challenges.

**MANAGER** - Growing cleaning and restoration company seeks person w/ experience & schooling in fire and water restoration for manager's position. Please send resume.

**ELEMENTARY SCHOOL PRINCIPAL** Elementary school principal for a public school district. Energetic and innovative. Needs to meet stateadministrative certification requirements. Prefer experience as an elementary principal.

**ASSISTANT EDITOR** - Assistant editor to be trained to become editor of a weekly paper. Must be flexible. Reporting, photography and copy editing involved. Send resume and clips.

**INSIDE SALES PERSON** - Inside sales person to take phone orders and solve customer problems. Must be energetic, organized, customer related.

**Figure 1–1.** Want Ads

Classified advertisements in daily newspapers not only provide listings of job opportunities, but also present the qualifications that employers are seeking in job applicants.

This advertisement is the most detailed in its listing of requirements. Are there any other unstated or implied requirements for the position? Should you interpret the advertisement to identify qualifications needed for that position?

As you look at the ad, you might ask what the employer means by communication skills. Because writing skills are mentioned as a separate requirement, you can infer that the company wants someone with good oral communication. Very likely, an executive secretary will be answering the telephone and relaying messages. Communication might also refer to interpersonal communication. An executive secretary will probably work with many people and must be able to get along well with others.

The ad's reference to the ability to handle multiple priorities, work independently, and take on new challenges all suggest that this is a busy office. If there are multiple priorities, it suggests that the secretary's workload might be heavy at times and this individual must be able to determine what needs to be done immediately and what can be put off for a while. If needed to work independently, it means that the boss also has a heavy workload and cannot spend much time explaining details. This organization is obviously looking for a secretary who is responsible, competent, and self-directed. Finally, if the secretary needs to be willing to take new challenges, it means that he or she must be able to handle any situation that might arise. Now let's look again at the advertisement for a manager.

### Manager

- Growing cleaning and restoration company seeks person w/ training and experience in fire and water restoration for manager's position.
- Please send resume.

Suppose you have worked in the housekeeping department of a hospital or a hotel; would you be considered for this job? Probably not, because what is involved here is not ordinary house cleaning. The applicant for this position needs to be able to demonstrate knowledge of how to clean and restore areas damaged by fire and water. Even experience in fire and water restoration would probably not be enough because the employer wants someone who has had training as well as experience.

This company is looking for a manager. Would you be considered for the position if you had no management experience? Perhaps, if you had the other qualifications, but you would have to be able to demonstrate your management potential. If you possessed the other required skills and could demonstrate responsibility and leadership, you might be a good candidate for the job even without prior management experience.

Let's move on to the ad for an elementary school principal.

### Elementary School Principal

- Elementary School Principal for a public school district.

- Energetic and innovative.

- Needs to meet state administrative certification requirements.

- Prefer experience as an elementary principal.

If you are about to graduate from college with a degree in elementary education, should you consider applying for the job of elementary principal? Don't waste your time! Before you would be considered for an administrative position in education, you will need at least a few years of experience as a teacher. In most states, this experience is part of the requirement for an administrative certificate.

What if you have a master's degree in elementary education and five years of experience as an elementary school teacher? Should you consider applying for the position when the ad states a preference for someone with experience as an elementary school principal? Sure! The employer would certainly consider you if you had those qualifications.

Can you demonstrate that you are energetic and innovative? Can you show that you have administrative and leadership ability—especially if you have no experience as an elementary school principal? If you can, you are a plausible candidate for this position. You can show administrative or leadership ability through committee work or work in professional organizations. A position such as department head or team leader will also demonstrate leadership and administrative ability.

Next, let's look at the ad for an assistant editor.

### Assistant Editor

- Assistant editor to be trained to become editor of a weekly newspaper.

- Must be flexible.

- Reporting, photography, and copy editing involved.

- Send resume and clips.

An assistant editor who will be trained to become the editor of this newspaper must be able to write, take photographs, and be skillful enough with the English language to edit the writing of other people. What other qualifications might be needed for this position? Unless this is strictly a one-person operation, the editor is going to need some management skills. The applicant for this job should definitely be able to show responsibility and initiative.

Finally, let's look at the ad for an inside sales person.

### Inside Sales Person

- Inside sales person to take phone orders and solve customer problems.
- Must be energetic, organized, customer related.

This ad calls for someone who is energetic, organized, and customer oriented; someone who is able to take telephone orders and solve customer problems. Some sales people need to be aggressive. Is aggressiveness a requirement for this position? Probably not, because it is inside sales where customers phone in orders. Perseverance is probably more important than aggressiveness in this position. The person selected for this position will have to persevere until the customer's problem is solved.

Because solving customer problems is one of the duties listed in this ad, there are likely to be many of problems to be solved. Perhaps the sales person frequently will have to deal with irate customers. If that's the situation, then the candidate for this job should be good at dealing with frustration. This individual will need to be calm and able to maintain his or her composure even if blamed for something over which he or she has no control. Tact and diplomacy will be important in this job. The candidate must be able to soothe a customer's anger and maintain the company's good will.

# ACTIVITY 1-1

The following eight ads were taken from the classified section of a newspaper. Read these ads and then answer the questions that follow.

**A.** Manager Trainee. New corp. expanding in the area. No exp. necessary. Will train in Mgmt, Marketing, & Sales. $11.00/hr. to start & bonuses. Hours flexible.

**B.** Exp. Restaurant Catering Manager.

**C.** Kitchen & Bath Designer. Experienced in sales and design. Strong outside sales experience a plus. Salary plus commissions.

**D.** Office Clerical. Full-time. Necessary skills fast typing, 65 WPM, and bookkeeping basics. Schedule includes 1 plus Sunday per month. No computers.

**E.** Ed Techs to work in behaviorally disordered/emotionally disturbed elementary classrooms in a psycho-educational day-treatment program. Must be able to set effective limits, assist teacher with elementary programs, and work effectively in treatment team approach. Experience strongly preferred. Send resume with cover letter.

**F.** Social Service. 60-bed ICF facility is currently accepting applications for the position of Social Service Director.

**G.** Grants Researcher/Writer, Freelance—for Arts Organization. $8–12/hr. depending on qualifications. Up to 300 hours in 1991. Self-starter, excellent research and writing skills. Resume and recent (nonfiction) writing samples.

**H.** Exciting opportunity. Self-starters. Potential of $500 to $900 per week selling ad space for local publications.

1. Which ads do not require any kind of experience? _____
_____
_____

2. Which ads would not require an ability to work extensively with other people? _____
_____
_____

3. Does ad F require previous experience? If so, what kind of experience would be appropriate? _____
_____
_____
_____

4. The pay for ad G depends on qualifications. What kind of qualifications is the employer looking for? _____
_____
_____
_____

5. Do any of these positions require a college degree? Explain. _____
_____
_____
_____

6. Ad E states that experience is strongly preferred. What kind of experience would be relevant to this position? _____
_____
_____
_____

7. Ad A is for manager trainees. What kind of management might this position involve? Is management skill the most important qualification for the position? Explain. _____
_____
_____
_____
_____

8. Choose two of the ads from this page and list all of the stated and unstated job requirements for the position. (Your instructor may ask you to bring in an actual classified ad from the newspaper or a job notice from another source.) _____
_____
_____
_____
_____
_____
_____
_____
_____
_____
_____
_____
_____

**Figure 1–2.** Ads Giving Little Information

Sometimes you learn about a job opening without learning the specific requirements for the position. Employment ads at times give very little information, as illustrated in Figure 1-2. When you see this kind of ad, you should analyze the position to discover the unstated job requirements. For example, any type of manager needs to be responsible and mature, in addition to being a good leader. Anyone doing virtually any kind of office work must be able to type, answer the telephone, and file. If the ad doesn't tell you anything about the job requirements, you have to think about the position so you can figure out what the job requirements are.

## FRIENDS

You might also learn about a job through another source—a friend, perhaps, who has little information about the specific job requirements. How do you determine the requirements in situations like these? You do essentially the same thing that you did when you looked beyond the requirements stated in the want ad. Normally, when you apply for a position, you know something about the duties involved in the job. If you are just graduating from school, however, and are interested in a particular career, yet don't know too much about it, you can find out. You might ask a teacher or someone who works in the field to tell you about its day-to-day duties. You might also look the job up for yourself in the *Encyclopedia of Careers and Vocational Guidance*. From your knowledge of what is expected of people in specific jobs, you analyze whether the job you are interested in is right for you.

What does a receptionist in a beauty salon or any other business do? She sets up appointments over the telephone, so she needs good oral communication skills. She greets customers when they come in and keeps track of their appointments, so she must be pleasant and well-organized. She may collect payment for services, so she should be accurate and responsible. She may even do some typing or record

Friends or acquaintances are often good sources of information about possible job opportunities.

keeping in between calls and customers, so she needs to have some clerical ability, although typing accuracy would be more important for her than speed.

Suppose that a friend who works for a social service agency tells you there is an opening for a social worker at her agency. What are the requirements for that position? If you are interested in doing social work, you probably already know that in most states, social workers are licensed and must have a college degree to get that license. You also probably know that social workers are skilled in working with people and need understanding, compassion, and patience. Because social workers have case loads dealing with many people, you should be able to organize your time and efforts as well. Social workers also write a lot of reports; therefore, you need to have good writing skills.

## JOB PLACEMENT AGENCIES

Another source of employment information is job placement agencies. Many schools and colleges have **placement offices** where students are brought together with prospective employers. Additionally, every state has employment agencies in its major cities, and every city has private employment agencies as well.

If you learn of a job opening through an employment agency, you will need to go through the same process you would go through if you learned about it through a want ad. What are the qualifications the employer is looking for? What can you do to demonstrate that you possess those qualifications?

Prospective employers often write to college placement offices to let them know about job openings. For example, the placement office at Casco Bay College recently received two letters soliciting applicants for a secretarial position. One of them told nothing about the job beyond the fact that it was a secretarial position. Any applicants who apply for this position will have to use their knowledge of what is involved in secretarial work so that they are able to demonstrate their qualifications.

Job placement agencies, run either by state or city authorities, are excellent sources of information regarding job opportunities and the qualifications necessary to apply for them.

The second letter was from a lawyer who wanted to hire a paralegal or legal secretary. In this letter, the lawyer indicated that the work involved mostly real estate and construction. This tells the job applicant that a course in real estate law would be an advantage in being considered for the job.

The letter also stated that the employer was looking for someone who was well-organized and efficient. This tells the job applicant that he or she will need to demonstrate organization and efficiency in his or her resume and cover letter.

Sometimes information about job openings is received by a college placement office by telephone rather than by letter. This gives the **employment counselor,**—who helps job seekers find appropriate openings, write resumes and cover letters, and prepare for the employment interview—a chance to ask for more details about the position. This information can then be passed on to any job applicants.

# ACTIVITY 1-2

The following three job notices came to Casco Bay College Placement Office by telephone. Read these ads and answer the questions that follow.

**A.** Excellent typing and organizational skills
IBM/WordPerfect
Financial records, telephone, correspondence,
bulk mailing, and general office

**B.** Legal Secretary with litigation experience a must
Computers
Very hectic, fast-paced office
Good personnel skills
Willing to help out

**C.** Small office—work for two attorneys
Word processing skills very important
Good phone skills, good organization skills
Dictaphone

1. In job notice A, is this opening primarily a secretarial or bookkeeping job?
   _____

2. Would the employer be looking for someone highly skilled in keeping financial records or would a general knowledge of financial record keeping be sufficient?
   _____
   _____
   _____

3. What could a job applicant do to show competence in that area?
   _____
   _____
   _____

4. How could a job applicant demonstrate organizational skills?
   _____
   _____
   _____
   _____

5. If a job applicant had never had any experience with bulk mailing, would it be a waste of time to apply for that position? Why or why not?

_____

_____

6. What is meant by personnel skills in job notice B?

_____

_____

7. What does the phrase "willing to help out" indicate about the job?

_____

_____

8. A student with excellent grades and two years of experience as a secretary in an insurance office is interested in this position. She has never worked in a law office before, but she has excellent references from her secretarial position. Should she apply for this job, or would it be a waste of time? Explain.

_____

_____

9. How would an applicant for job notice C demonstrate telephone skills if he or she had never worked at a job that involved answering the telephone?

_____

_____

**Figure 1–3.** Classified Advertisements

The first step in preparing your resume, then, is to review the specific requirements of the job in which you are interested. It doesn't matter whether you learned about the job from a classified ad, from a friend who knows about a job opening, from a placement office, or whether you contacted the company yourself and learned that there was a position available. You determine the qualifications needed by looking at the stated requirements and by analyzing the position to discover the unstated requirements.

Read between the lines of a want ad or job notice to gain an understanding of the unstated job requirements. If an ad says something like "self-starter," you can be sure that the company wants someone who demonstrates responsibility and independence. If an employer wants someone to "coordinate the work flow in a busy office," you know that they are looking for someone who is well-organized. If a job notice asks for a manager, you know that the job calls for someone with experience in the field and leadership ability, although not necessarily management experience. (See Figure 1-3.)

Use your education and your knowledge of the job to analyze the position. If you're still unsure as to what might be involved in a particular kind of job, ask a teacher, a counselor, or someone who has worked in the field. If you still need more information, go to the library and research the career in the *Encyclopedia of Careers and Vocational Guidance*. Once you have discovered the job requirements and measured your ability to meet them with your qualifications, you are ready for the second step—preparing an inventory of your qualifications for the position.

# ACTIVITY 1-3

List some of the major requirements that might be requested for the following jobs:

1. Entry-level electronics technician

   _____

   _____

   _____

2. Sales manager

   _____

   _____

   _____

3. Payroll clerk

   _____

   _____

   _____

4. Customer service representative in a bank

   _____

   _____

   _____

5. Purchasing agent

   _____

   _____

   _____

6. Paramedic

   _____

   _____

   _____

7. Paralegal

   _____

   _____

   _____

8. Public relations officer

   _____

   _____

   _____

9. Management trainee large insurance company

   _____

   _____

   _____

10. Travel agent

    _____

    _____

    _____

11. List the requirements for a job that interests you.

    _____

    _____

    _____

## PREPARE AN INVENTORY OF YOUR QUALIFICATIONS

Your qualifications for any job are primarily your education and your experience. Bear in mind, however, that your education is not the piece of paper that says you are a bachelor of arts or science, but what you learned while earning your degree. What you learned includes what you experienced in extra-curricular activities as well as what you learned in class.

### WORK EXPERIENCE

Sometimes people think that they have no experience, but no adult has "no experience." An individual may have no experience as an accountant or an engineer, but he or she may have worked as a cashier, a short-order cook, or a filling station attendant. All jobs teach us valuable work habits. Any job we have held has taught us such characteristics as reliability, responsibility, cooperation, and the ability to work with the public. Whether you are just graduating from college or simply changing careers, you can use your past work experience to demonstrate some of the skills, aptitudes, and personal characteristics that will be required in the job for which you are applying.

### VOLUNTEER EXPERIENCE

Your experience includes more than the jobs you have held; it also includes volunteer work. In volunteer work, you may have learned skills or demonstrated abilities that you have not used in any paid work activity. These qualities can be especially helpful if you have been an officer of any organization or if you headed a committee or otherwise demonstrated leadership. Anything you have done in the way of **volunteer work** (work for which one is not paid, but that provides special skills or relevant job experiences) with a philanthropic, social, or school organization, a religious group, or a political group may enhance your candidacy for a job.

### PERSONAL ATTRIBUTES

Still another qualification that you bring to a job is your **personal attributes**, which are personal qualities such as leadership, communication skill, or organizational ability. What kind of person are you? Are you creative? Do you have initiative? Are you friendly? Are you determined? Well-organized? Analytical? Are you a leader? Do you express your ideas well in writing? In speaking? Do you understand people? Do people respond well to you? Do you learn quickly? Do you persevere? Are you accurate? Fair-minded? Honest? What other personal attributes do you have?

Once you have drawn up an **inventory of qualifications**, or list of your qualifications for a particular job, you need to match them against any job that you might be considering. For example, an ad for a data entry/payroll person asks for a quality-conscious, detail-oriented individual, someone with excellent communication and problem-solving skills, a person who would be comfortable interacting with customers. As you can see, knowledge of payroll and data entry by themselves are not enough for this job. The company is looking for a candidate with all kinds of personal attributes as well. You need to be sure that you have the personal attributes as well as the technical skills for any job for which you want to apply.

# ACTIVITY 1-4

Draw up a list of your qualifications for a job.

1. SPECIAL SKILLS (Special skills would include things like knowledge of a foreign language or ability to operate any kind of machinery. Things like typing speed or shorthand speed would also be included here.)

   _____     _____
   _____     _____
   _____     _____
   _____     _____

2. EDUCATION AND TRAINING

   _____     _____
   _____     _____
   _____     _____
   _____     _____

3. EXPERIENCE

   _____     _____
   _____     _____
   _____     _____
   _____     _____

4. SPECIAL QUALIFICATIONS SUCH AS HONORS, ACTIVITIES, AND MEMBERSHIPS

   _____     _____
   _____     _____
   _____     _____
   _____     _____

5. PERSONAL ATTRIBUTES (Don't be modest.)

   _____     _____
   _____     _____
   _____     _____
   _____     _____
   _____     _____

---

**HELP WANTED**

EXECUTIVE SECRETARY - Excellent secretarial skills, including typing (70 wpm), shorthand (100 wpm) and word processing. Excellent writing, communication and organizational skills. Ability to handle multiple priorities and complete special assignments independently. Ability to work efficiently and the desire to take on new challenges.

**Figure 1–4.** Want Ad From Daily Newspaper

## DEMONSTRATING YOUR QUALIFICATIONS

Once you have completed this inventory of qualifications, you should ask yourself how you can demonstrate each one of them. You feel that you are well-organized and analytical and that you have leadership ability. Can you demonstrate these qualities? Can you offer some evidence? What have you done that required organizational ability? What have you done that required an analytical mind? What have you analyzed? Whom have you led? Answers to questions like these will demonstrate your personal characteristics.

Let's take another look at our advertisement for an executive secretary (see Figure 1–4).

The employer wants a person who, among other qualities, possesses excellent writing, communication, and organizational skills. If you have worked as an executive secretary previously, you can use your past experience to demonstrate your capabilities. However, what if you have no secretarial experience? Your writing skill can be demonstrated in both your resume and cover letter. You can be sure that the employer will review your resume and accompanying letter very carefully. As noted earlier, communication skills can mean both oral communi-

**Figure 1–5.** Want Ad From Daily Newspaper

cation and interpersonal communication. A volunteer position that included answering the telephone might demonstrate oral communication, as would a college course in this subject. Working with the public as a cashier or a waitress may demonstrate an ability to get along with people, or interpersonal communication. Organizing or heading a committee or a project can demonstrate an ability to organize.

Let's also revisit our ad for an elementary principal who is energetic and innovative (see Figure 1–5).

How do you demonstrate these attributes? To demonstrate that you are energetic, you must show that you participate in a number of activities. Perhaps you are a member of several professional and social organizations and, possibly, you hold an office in one of them. You may have written articles for professional journals or have been involved in some special projects in education or in civic organizations. The fact that you are a member of the local garden club by itself will not enhance your candidacy for the position. However, combining this activity with other memberships and activities will demonstrate that you are energetic and outgoing. If, on the other hand, you submit a resume that shows little more than a degree in education, a certain number of years' experience as an elementary teacher, and membership in two or three professional organizations, your qualifications will not seem very impressive. Belonging to two or three organizations will not be overly impressive because most teachers belong to several. To belong, all you have to do is pay your dues. You don't even have to go to the meetings.

What might you do to demonstrate that you are innovative? Instead of writing:

Taught 5th grade at XYZ School from 1984 to present,

you might write:

- Developed new program to help students with reading problems. Class advanced 1-1/2 years in reading level.

- Initiated math tutorial with faster students helping those who needed extra help.

The point is, when you draw up an inventory of your qualifications, you have to relate them to the specific job requirements. You should determine what your qualifications are, which qualifications are relevant to the job you are applying for, and finally, how you can demonstrate on paper that you actually have the qualifications you say you have.

# ACTIVITY 1-5

Look back at your list of personal attributes in Activity 1-4. To the right of that list write something that would demonstrate that you actually possess each one of those personal attributes.

On your resume, in your cover letter, and in every phase of your job search, you want to appear confident, but not boastful or pompous. Not only do most people find boastfulness and pomposity offensive, but the boastful terms we use are usually not convincing. Boastful statements are usually generalities. You communicate the same message much more convincingly without seeming to boast if, instead of relying on empty generalities, you use specifics. Remember, your qualifications for a position are based on what you have already accomplished, not on your opinion of yourself. Some resumes have a section titled

SUCCESSFUL RESUMES AND INTERVIEWS

Personal Qualifications. Under this section people will list adjectives such as *bright, cheerful, hard-working*, or *competent*. These are empty statements. They carry no weight, will convince no employer, and sound boastful. It's much better to demonstrate these characteristics through specifics. You think you're hard-working and bright. What makes you think so, and how can you demonstrate these qualities to an employer? You can write:

> Worked full-time while attending college full-time and graduated with honors.

Anyone who did these things would have to be both hard-working and bright.

What about cheerfulness? It's a very subjective quality. Although most employers would rather have employees with pleasant personalities, cheerfulness itself is not a qualification for many jobs. It may be best to forget about this.

Competence? What does that mean? Does the person who says he is competent mean it in a general sense? Can it be demonstrated? Does it mean competence in the sense of specific skills relating to the job? If that is what is meant, then it would be better to demonstrate competence in those specific skills.

# ACTIVITY 1-6

Figure 1–6 provides job notices taken from classified ads and placement office postings. Read these ads and then answer the questions that follow.

**ACCOUNTANT** Prominent local property management company has an opening for an accounting clerk. Must have PC Computer skills, accounting/bookkeeper experience, and ability to work in a fast-paced, dynamic organization. Send resume and wage requirement.

**AVIATION CUSTOMER SERVICE** Immediate opening for an exciting position at the Jetport. Duties include: greeting customers and coordinating aircraft services with ramp personnel. Successful candidate will have strong organization skills and be familiar with Portland community. Some bookkeeping experience helpful. Some evening and weekend work.

**CLERK** Immediate opening for position with Maine Superior Court. An entry-level position that involves extensive contact with the public and legal professionals. Duties include typing (at least 45 wpm), record keeping, and responding to the public. Requires a high school diploma or equivalent, with experience in office procedures a definite plus. Send resume.

**CAD OPERATOR** To produce fabrication drawings on Autocad 10. Familiarity with industrial process machinery a plus. Strong mechanical aptitude required. Ideal candidate will be able to provide telephone technical support for the products drawn.

**RETAIL MERCHANDISER** Service retail customers for national distributor. Stock and reorder merchandise. No sales. Experience helpful but will train.

**PROGRAM COORDINATOR** For practical life skills program. Serving 52 adults with developmental disabilities. Responsibilities include development and facilitation of Individual Program Plans, case management, supervision of staff. Bachelor's degree in a related field. Good writing skills a must. Send resume.

**INSIDE TECHNICAL SALES PERSON** Excellent communication skills, strong mechanical aptitude and familiarity with IBM spreadsheet and word processor applications required. Familiarity with industrial process machinery a plus. Duties include costing for custom-built products, customer service, technical consultation, correspondence. Send resume.

**ASSISTANT** For growing property management firm. Must enjoy wide variety of tasks, bookkeeping, showing apts, recording rents, tenant interaction. Computer knowledge of Lotus, Acct/Payable & WordPerfect helpful. Send resume.

**MACHINIST 1ST CLASS** Candidate must have experience in short run precision prototype work. Call or write.

**COLLECTIONS** Person to handle commercial collections. Must have proven success record in reducing A/R diplomatically. Call for details.

**RN LPN** We need a few good people to join our family. We offer holistic nursing care. Progressive health care through case management and team approach. If you are looking for a new and exciting opportunity in nursing, call today for an appointment.

**DENTAL HYGIENIST** Looking for an enthusiastic, organized, loyal team player. Education, communication, and the delivery of high quality hygiene services are some of our goals. Send resume.

**ASSISTANT MANAGER** Qualifications: Bilingual in English and French. Bachelors Degree in Business Administration or Accounting, knowledge and experience in loan portfolio and secondary mortgage market a plus. Send letter and resume.

**DRAFTER** Seeking a full-time Architectural Drafter with CAD experience. Send resume.

**SHIPPER** Busy warehouse. Send resume.

**KIT MGR/WORKING COOK** Responsible for all aspects of kitchen operation. Send resume.

**DATA ANALYST** Responsibilities include 1) Analysis of routine reports 2) Working with various departments to develop new reports 3) Installation of new hardware and software for PCs. Requirements include a bachelor's degree, strong working knowledge of Lotus 123 & DBase III, familiarity with PCs, strong analytical skills, and good communications skills. Experience in a health care environment would be a plus.

**ENGLISH TEACHER** For a one year course in composition beginning in the fall. Teaching experience necessary. Send resume to Bedford College.

**Figure 1–6.** Classified Advertisements

1. From the preceding job notices, choose a notice for a position that interests you. Then make a list of the stated and unstated requirements for the job you chose.

_____
_____
_____
_____
_____
_____

2. Make a list of your qualifications for the position.

_____
_____
_____
_____
_____

3. For each qualification you have listed, give some evidence to demonstrate that you possess that qualification.

_____
_____
_____
_____
_____
_____

# SOFTWARE APPLICATION 1

Use this application to help you learn how to identify specific job requirements from advertisements. Practice is provided in determining job requirements by reviewing stated requirements, then analyzing the position to discover its unstated requirements, and then creating itemized lists.

# SOFTWARE APPLICATION 2

Use this application to review the process of drawing up an inventory of your job qualifications and beginning the process of presenting evidence of those qualifications. After completing this application, you will be ready to prepare the elements of your resume.

# Writing a Successful Resume

**OBJECTIVES**

**After you have studied this chapter, you should be able to:**

- **Write an effective career objective on your resume.**

- **Use your resume to show how your education contributes to your qualifications for a position.**

- **List your experience on your resume so that it speaks *persuasively* about your qualifications.**

- **Use the other parts of your resume to show how your personal attributes help qualify you for a position.**

- **Write a resume that is attractive, readable, persuasive, concise, and focused.**

As they begin to draft their resumes, some people find it helpful to use the new computer software that is available for resume writing. Some computer software gives the job seeker information about different types of jobs. Other software helps applicants review their strengths and weaknesses as they consider different careers.

Some software actually helps people draft their resumes, using different formats to emphasize different areas of their qualifications. Other software packages can be used to create chronological, functional, or combined resumes. Some even contain lists of active verbs to help users strengthen their resumes.

Whether you use a computer or typewriter to develop your own resume, you should understand what makes one resume succeed while another fails. In the next few pages you will see the characteristics of a winning resume.

## THE CHARACTERISTICS OF A WINNING RESUME

A resume allows an employer to see at a glance what your main qualifications are for a job. "At a glance" is a key phrase here. It means that your resume must be brief—a page, a page-and-a-half, never more than two pages. It also means that your resume must be set up in such a way that it will be easy to read.

From your point of view, your resume is an opportunity to present your qualifications in the best possible light. This means that you will not include everything you have ever done. Everything that you do include on your resume will have the purpose of revealing one of your qualifications. Further, your resume will be set up and phrased in such a way that it will emphasize those qualifications that relate to the position for which you are applying.

With these points in mind, let's consider the five characteristics of a winning resume: *attractiveness, readability, persuasiveness, conciseness,* and *focus.*

A resume both allows an employer to review a job applicant's qualifications at a glance and provides an applicant with an opportunity to present his or her qualifications in the best possible light.

## ATTRACTIVENESS

To impress an employer, your resume has to look good. It must be 8 1/2 by 11 inches in size; it should be on good quality paper (one that shows typing or printing well); it has to be free of typos and other errors; and it needs to be laid out cleanly and attractively.

There is no one correct format for a resume. In the model resumes that will be used in this book, several different formats are used so that you can decide for yourself which format appeals to you and serves your purposes best.

## READABILITY

Your resume should not be jumbled together in paragraph form. It should be set up so that the employer can see your qualifications at a glance. Leave white space between sections, and, instead of paragraphs, use a series of verb phrases arranged for readability.

Compare the following:

> I opened the store in the morning, arranged merchandise on display shelves, and kept track of inventory. After six months, I was promoted to assistant manager. After my promotion, I began filling out daily sales reports. I also trained new employees.

- Arranged merchandise
- Kept track of inventory
- Promoted to assistant manager after six months
- Filled out daily sales reports
- Trained new employees

The second version is more readable, doesn't take any more space, and contains about the same amount of information as the first. In the first version, opening the store in the morning shows something about this person. The manager must have considered this employee responsible and reliable to trust her with the keys. In the second version, however, the promotion to assistant manager shows the same thing and more. If this individual hadn't been promoted to assistant manager, it would have been helpful for her to have included a remark in the second version about opening the store in the morning.

## PERSUASIVENESS

The person from whom we borrowed a portion of the resume in the previous section might have said that she was creative, accurate, responsible, reliable, and competent. She did not use these terms, however, because they are general statements, and general statements are not persuasive. The applicant did not need to use these generalizations because specific listings of her job responsibilities demonstrated her abilities.

She did not have to say that she was creative. Instead, she told us something that she did that demonstrated creative ability: arranged merchandise. She kept track of inventory and filled out daily sales reports. These duties both require accuracy. If she had not been reliable, responsible, and competent, she would not have been promoted and she would not have been allowed to train new employees.

Adjectives describing your capabilities carry no weight and are not persuasive. If you want your resume to be persuasive, you need to use a series of phrases that begin with active verbs such as supervised, directed, developed, managed, established, or initiated. These phrases will be persuasive because they show what you have already done.

## CONCISENESS

Your resume is a summary. It presents your main qualifications. It must be brief and to the point. As we noted earlier, it should be no more than a page to a page-and-a-half. If your resume is too long, a busy executive might not take the time to read it, especially if there are dozens of other resumes for the same job.

## FOCUS

When we discussed qualifications for a position in Chapter 1, we emphasized that qualifications included everything you learned in school, every job you've ever held, every duty you performed and skills you learned on that job, every organization you belonged to, every activity you participated in, and every personal characteristic you might possess. Most job seekers have dozens, if not hundreds, of specific qualifications for positions for which they are applying.

How can you possibly get all of those qualifications on one or two pages? The answer is that you don't try to get *everything* on your resume. You select those qualifications that relate to the position for which you are applying and emphasize those in your resume.

In selecting and emphasizing those characteristics that are most relevant to the kind of job for which you are applying, you are focusing your resume. (See Figure 2-1.)

---

**FRED ST CLAIR**
1236 Broad Street
Youngstown, Ohio 44501
(216) 555-1244

**OBJECTIVE**

Seeking a position as a social worker

**SUPERVISING AND ORGANIZATION**

* Supervised house staff at residence for people with handicaps
* Developed program to prepare handicapped workers for community employment
* Counseled clients in Work Adjustment Program at Goodwill of Ohio
* Developed jobs in the community for Goodwill clients who were job ready
* Coordinated annual job Placement Seminar at Lima High for three years
* History Department Head, Lima High School

**EXPERIENCE**

| | |
|---|---|
| 1987–present | Goodwill of Ohio, Youngstown OH, Counselor and House Manager |
| 1981–1987 | Lima High School, Lima OH, History Teacher and Department Head |
| 1977–1981 | Bowling Green High School, Bowling Green OH, History Teacher |

**EDUCATION**

Ohio State University, M. Ed., 1981. Major: Education
Findlay College B.A., 1977. Major: History

**MEMBERSHIPS**

National Writers Club
National Rehabilitation Association

---

**Figure 2–1.** A Model Resume

# GENERAL PURPOSE VS. FOCUSED RESUMES

There may be situations where you are qualified for several different jobs in one general field. In this situation, you might be tempted to prepare a **general purpose resume** that can be sent out with applications for more than one type of job.

In most instances, however, you will be better served not to use a general purpose resume for several purposes. It will be more effective to prepare more than one resume, each focused toward a specific position or situation.

For example, let's say a young man is graduating from college with a major in history. He has no interest in a career in teaching. He majored in history because he enjoyed it. Now he has to work for a living and he thinks he would like to work in business, perhaps in management or sales—he's not sure which.

He could develop a general purpose resume that would show his general qualifications. He must be intelligent; he graduated from college. He probably has some kind of work experience that would demonstrate that he is dependable and reliable, and so forth.

The truth is, this young man is not very qualified for the careers in which he is interested. He has no training or direct experience in either management or sales. This doesn't necessarily mean that no company would consider hiring him. His college degree would indicate that he has potential, and many businesses would be willing to give him the specific on-the-job training that he needs to become a productive employee.

Because this young man doesn't have the training or experience, however, he would more likely be selected for an **entry-level,** or starting, **position** in management or sales if he could demonstrate that he possesses at least the personal attributes required for the job. He would be better served, then, if he prepared two resumes—one for a management trainee position and one for a position in sales.

If he has done anything that demonstrated leadership, he should include it on his management resume. Was he elected to office in any organization he belonged to? Did he head any kind of committee? Did he ever initiate a new procedure at any job he held? Management involves responsibility, initiative, and organizational ability as well as leadership, so anything he did that demonstrated any of these qualifications should be listed on this resume. In the part-time and summer jobs that he has held, where did he show responsibility? Where did he see something that needed to be done and go ahead and do it or, even better, get a group of people to do it? Better still, how was he recognized for his initiative? In what way did he organize either his own activities or a group of people in an activity?

If our history major were preparing a resume for a sales career, he would emphasize other qualifications. Has he worked with the public? Does he have good oral communication skills? What has he done to demonstrate this? Does he have a pleasant personality? How can he demonstrate this? Has he been elected to an office in any organization? Has he been involved in a number of campus activities? Is he good at solving problems? Would he be able to solve customers' problems? These are the kinds of qualities he would want to emphasize on his resume if he were interested in a career in sales. If you look at Owen Strait's resumes in Figures 2-2 and 2-3, you will see how this works.

Both of these are **functional resumes**, which allow an applicant to present his or her qualifications in skill clusters. Owen chose a functional resume so that he could present his qualifications in skill clusters. **Skill clusters** are groups of activities that demonstrate particular qualifications. The resume in Figure 2-2 is geared toward sales. Because a sales person needs to work well with people and to solve problems, Owen drew up a resume with skill clusters that demonstrated his ability in these two areas.

The resume in Figure 2-3 is geared toward management. The Experience section of this resume emphasizes Owen's leadership and organizational skills

# OWEN STRAIT

217 Amherst Street
Livonia, NY 14487
(716) 555-7720

## Objective

Seeking a sales position

## EXPERIENCE

### PROBLEM SOLVING

* Advertising Director, *The Albany*, student newspaper
  Reorganized procedures and doubled sales in one year
* Shift Leader, McDonald's, Albany, NY, 199_–9_
  Implemented new procedure for inventory control

### WORKING WITH PEOPLE

* 2nd Lieutenant, U.S. Army, The Infantry School, Fort Benning, GA, Jul–Dec 199_
* Vice-President, Sigma Tau Gamma, SUNY, Albany, NY 199_–9_
* Captain, Albany Rangers Basketball Team, 199_–9_
* Order taker, McDonald's, Albany, NY 199_–9_
* Shift leader, McDonald's, Albany, NY 199_–9_
  Earned enough to pay for most living expenses at college

## EDUCATION

Graduated from the Leadership Course, The Infantry
   School, Fort Benning, GA, Dec. 199_
B.A., History, SUNY, Albany, NY, May 199_

## HONORS AND ACTIVITIES

Honor Graduate, Leadership Course, The Infantry School
Outstanding ROTC graduate, SUNY, Albany, NY
Member, Interfraternity Council, SUNY, Albany, NY
Member, White Water Rafting Club

## REFERENCES: Furnished upon Request

Figure 2–2. Owen Strait's Functional Resume Geared Toward Sales

# OWEN STRAIT

217 Amherst Street
Livonia, NY 14487
(716) 555-7720

## Objective

Seeking a position as management trainee

## EXPERIENCE

## LEADERSHIP

* 2nd Lieutenant, U.S. Army, The Infantry School, Ft. Benning, GA, Jul–Dec 199_
* Vice-President, Sigma Tau Gamma, SUNY, Albany, NY 199_–9_
* President, Sigma Tau Gamma, SUNY, Albany, NY, 199_–9_
* Shift Leader, McDonald's, Albany, NY, 199_–9_
* Captain of Albany Rangers Basketball Team, 199_–9_

## ORGANIZATIONAL ABILITY

* Organized Homecoming activities, Sigma Tau Gamma, SUNY, Albany, NY
* Reorganized advertising department of college newspaper and doubled advertising sales
* Implemented new inventory procedure at McDonald's, Albany, NY

## EDUCATION

Graduated from the Leadership Course, The Infantry School, Fort Benning, GA,
    Dec. 199_
B.A., History, SUNY, Albany, NY, May 199_

## HONORS AND ACTIVITIES

Honor Graduate, Leadership Course, The Infantry School
Outstanding ROTC graduate, SUNY, Albany, NY
Leadership Award, Livonia High School, Livonia, NY
Advertising Director, *The Albany*, student newspaper
Member, Interfraternity Council, SUNY, Albany, NY
Member, White Water Rafting Club

## REFERENCES: Furnished upon Request

**Figure 2–3.** Owen Strait's Functional Resume Geared Toward Management

because both of these would be important in management. He also included his high school leadership award under Honors and Activities of this resume because it demonstrated leadership.

# ACTIVITY 2-1

Write down your first and second choices for a career. Under each choice list your major qualifications for that career.

### CAREER CHOICES

First _____     Second _____

### Qualifications

_____     _____
_____     _____
_____     _____
_____     _____
_____     _____
_____     _____

## THE PARTS OF YOUR RESUME

A typical resume contains six or seven sections. A heading tells a prospective employer how to get in touch with you; an objective explains what kind of job you are looking for; and experience and education present your major qualifications. Most resumes also contain a section that tells about your activities, honors, awards, memberships, and skills. Some resumes contain an interest section as well that tells a prospective employer about some of the things you enjoy doing away from the job. Finally, most resumes say something about how your references can be obtained.

### HEADING

Your name, address, and telephone number will appear at the top of your resume. Do not include the word "Resume" because it will be obvious what this sheet of paper is. One of the characteristics of a good resume is conciseness. You don't want any superfluous information on your resume, and pointing out the obvious is superfluous information.

If you are a college student or for any reason live at a temporary address, you might want to include both your permanent and your temporary addresses. If you do this, you should indicate the last date you expect to be at your temporary address and the first date you expect to be at your permanent address.

You also must provide a telephone number, a place where you can be reached, on your resume. If you don't have a telephone, give a number where people would be willing to take messages for you.

### OBJECTIVE

Your heading should be followed by a statement of your career **objective**. This statement immediately shows the people in a personnel office what kind of job you are looking for. Occasionally, you'll find a resume that does not include such a statement. My recommendation, however, is to state your objective.

"Mr. Cartwright says you have to make a career decision—African violets or accounting."

Drawing by H. Martin; © 1990, The New Yorker Magazine, Inc.

When you write your statement, remember that you are summarizing your career objective for a prospective employer, not for yourself. Don't tell an employer that you plan to go to graduate school full-time in three years or that you expect to start your own business after you have had a few years' experience. Your statement of objective should match the description of the job for which you are applying.

If you are applying for only one job and making only one copy of your resume, you should tailor your statement of career objective specifically to fit that position. Most often, however, you will send out more than one copy of your resume while job hunting. This means that you should keep your statement of objective fairly general. You do not want to describe your ideal job in your objective because you might close the door to another position that may not be ideal but that would be perfectly acceptable to you.

Can you see why the following statement of objective would not be in an applicant's best interest?

OBJECTIVE: Seeking an entry-level position as an accountant in large firm that would give me significant responsibility and an opportunity to rise to mid-management level within three years.

This statement will close more doors than it will open. First of all, it would be pointless to send a resume with this statement to a small- or medium-sized company. Second, few large companies will move anyone from an entry-level position to mid-management in three years. It would be more effective for an applicant to make a more general statement of objective:

OBJECTIVE: Seeking an entry-level position in accounting.

# ACTIVITY 2-2

In the space provided below, write your statement of career objective.

_____

_____

_____

Now take a careful look at your statement.

1.  Do you have the qualifications to achieve your career objective?

_____

2.  Is your statement sufficiently general that you could put it on resumes going to different companies, both large and small?

_____

3.  Is there anything in your statement that might close some doors to you?

_____

4.  Does your statement tell a prospective employer anything about your future plans that might stand in the way of your being considered for a job?

_____

_____

5.  Look at your statement of objective from an employer's point of view. If you were the employer and you had available the kind of opening that is being sought, would you read the rest of the resume or would you stop there?

_____

_____

6.  After you have asked yourself these questions, you might want to revise your statement of objective. Here is a place to do it.
    Revised Statement of Objective:

_____

_____

## EDUCATION

After you have stated your career objective, you will begin listing your qualifications for a position. If you are a recent college graduate, your major qualification will be your degree, so you should list your education first. If, on the other hand, you have had extensive experience in the job market, you should list your experience before you list your education.

If you have attended more than one college, you should list your education in reverse chronological order beginning with the last college you attended.

Some resumes include high school education. This is not usually recommended unless you have never been to college. If you have gone to college for even one semester, you must have graduated from high school or earned a GED. In other words, the fact that you have graduated from high school is superfluous information. You want to keep your resume concise. If you had some unusual distinction in high school, if you were the valedictorian of your graduating class, for example, you might include that information under another section of your resume without listing your high school under the education section.

In the education section, you can include shorter training courses, workshops, seminars, courses in the military, and individual courses that did not lead toward a degree if they are relevant to the position for which you are applying. This information might be helpful on your resume if you have limited formal education in the field for which you are seeking employment. Let's say, for example, that you are graduating from college with a degree in liberal arts. You worked one summer selling encyclopedias. As part of that job, you had a one-week training session in sales techniques. If you are applying for a job in sales, you should not only list the job as part of your experience, you should also list the training session as part of your education.

The section on education primarily will include your college education. You need to list the college from which you graduated, your major and your minor, if any, and your degree and date of graduation. If you have not yet graduated, you should write:

Candidate for B.A. in Social Welfare, Hedgewick College, June 1990.

Other information that you might include under education could be your class standing, your overall grade point average (GPA), or your grade point average in your major. These should be included only if your grades are good and only if you are a recent graduate or still in college. Good grades are often taken to be indicators of future success. If you have professional experience and your resume is rather sparse, you can give it substance by listing some of the courses in your major that are relevant to the position for which you are applying. Any special projects or unusual educational experiences may be included here as well. Internships should go under experience rather than education.

# ACTIVITY 2-3

1.  List your post-secondary education, including degree, major, college, and date of graduation. If you have attended more than one college, list the colleges in reverse chronological order. If you have never taken any college courses, list your high school and date of graduation.

    _____
    _____
    _____
    _____

2.  List any special courses, training, seminars workshops, etc., that relate to your career objective.

    _____
    _____
    _____
    _____

3.  If you do not have much to put on your resume and you are just graduating from school, list the important courses in your major.

    _____    _____
    _____    _____
    _____    _____
    _____    _____

## EXPERIENCE

The way your experience is presented on your resume depends on whether you are creating a standard (chronological resume or a functional (skills) resume. On a standard resume, your work experience is listed in reverse chronological order. On a functional resume, your work experience is arranged in clusters of different skills. For example, one of your clusters might be organizational skills. Under this heading you should list any job or duty where you exercised organizational ability. Here is an example of the way a section of a functional resume might be set up to demonstrate organizational ability.

### Organizational Ability

- Coordinated the work flow in a busy office
- Planned the schedules and supervised the activities of five employees
- Prepared and coordinated monthly department head meetings
- Reorganized procedures in the billing department

Whether you use a standard or a functional resume should depend on your particular situation. A standard resume lists your experience, starting with your most recent job and working backward. A functional resume lists your experience in skill clusters. Owen Strait's resumes in Figures 2-2 and 2-3 are examples of functional resumes. In most situations, a standard resume is the best to use. If you have little experience in the field in which you are interested, however, you can use a functional resume to demonstrate your skills in that field.

People sometimes wonder how much of their work experience should be listed on their resumes. How far back should you go? Should every job be included? Suppose you were fired from a job? Should you include that job on your resume? The answers to those questions vary according to your situation. The resume of a recent college graduate will differ from that of an individual with several years of work experience. There will also be a difference between the resume of someone making a career change and that of someone seeking a different job in the same field.

The experience section of a resume is usually the most important part, especially for someone with an extensive work background. Whether you have professional experience or not, this section of your resume is going to paint a picture of the kind of employee you are. You want to present the image of a steady, reliable worker. To answer one of the questions from a previous paragraph, being fired from a job is not a reason to leave that job out of your resume, particularly if that omission will make a significant gap in your employment history. You don't want the prospective employer to wonder what you were doing during those years that are missing.

A functional resume can cover up gaps in employment, but it may also cause an alert employer to wonder if you are using this type of resume for just such a purpose. If you have a good, steady employment record and you want to use the experience clusters of a functional resume to emphasize your skills, you may want to prepare a **combined resume**, which has a chronological record of employment along with experience clusters.

Let's look again at the question of how much of your work experience should be included on your resume. If you are just graduating from college, you probably have no experience in the type of job for which you are applying. But most people, by the time they graduate, have worked summers or part-time during the school year. On these jobs people show responsibility, dependability, communication skills in working with people, and organizational skills. Many of these

Part-time and summer jobs offer job seekers valuable experience in fields in which they wish to build careers as well as providing them with real-world experience that can be used on their resumes.

skills, and certainly the knowledge of how to function on a job, might be valuable in the job for which you are applying.

If you have no professional experience, list your part-time and summer jobs. You don't have to include every part-time job you've had since you were 16; just include the most significant ones—the ones where you worked the longest, had the highest level of responsibility, or where you worked several summers in a row.

After you have worked professionally, of course, you no longer need to list these part-time jobs on your resume. If you have worked on one job as a secretary for one year, that experience demonstrates not only the specific skills required for the job but also the personal attributes that all employers look for in their employees such as reliability, acceptance of responsibility, and ability to take direction and to get along with co-workers.

How far back should you go in listing your work experience? The answer is simple: Go all the way back. If you have worked in a career for 25 years, you have a lot of valuable experience. There is no reason to include only the last 10 years of it.

What about people changing careers? Career changers should list all of their professional experience. Even though they are changing professions, they have doubtlessly acquired skills in one career that will be useful in another. These individuals might want to use a functional or a combination resume to emphasize those skills.

# ACTIVITY 2-4

In the space provided below, list your significant employment in reverse chronological order. Include job title, employers' names, dates of employment, and significant duties or contributions that you made to the company for which you worked.

_____

_____

_____

_____

_____

_____

_____

_____

_____

_____

_____

## MAKING THE EXPERIENCE SECTION OF YOUR RESUME MORE PERSUASIVE

Some people use adjectives on their resume to describe their capabilities, but adjectives are not persuasive. To persuade a prospective employer of your capabilities, you need to use phrases that begin with **active verbs** (verbs that show action). For example, if you feel you are reliable, you might write a phrase indicating something that you have done which reveals reliability, such as:

Cashed up and closed the shop one night a week.

# ACTIVITY 2-5

Turn the following adjectives into verb phrases that demonstrate the capability which the adjective describes.

EXAMPLE

| | |
|---|---|
| creative | Developed new method of handling returns |
| responsible | _____ |
| energetic | _____ |
| accurate | _____ |
| capable | _____ |
| hard-working | _____ |
| fast | _____ |
| competent | _____ |

## ACTIVITIES, HONORS, AWARDS, MEMBERSHIPS, AND SKILLS

Although there is no section on a resume entitled "Miscellaneous," there may be miscellaneous sections that can highlight activities, honors, awards, memberships, and skills. The title you give this section depends on what you want to emphasize. For example, if you received some academic awards in college and belonged to a number of college or professional organizations, you might call this section "Awards and Memberships." If you played collegiate sports and served on one or two committees, you might call this section "Activities."

Some careers might call for something special in this section. If you are a college professor, you might list professional publications here. If you are in the field of travel and tourism, you might list foreign and domestic travel.

A miscellaneous section on your resume can reveal something about your personal qualities that an employer might find attractive or impressive. If you are involved in a number of outside activities, you are more likely to be involved and energetic on the job as well. If you have received academic honors, you are probably bright and hard-working. If you are an officer in an organization, you probably get along well with people, are perceived by others as being responsible, and may be a natural leader. If you belong to professional organizations, you show an active interest in your chosen field.

# ACTIVITY 2-6

In the space provided below, list any activities, memberships, or honors that you have been awarded. This is especially important if you are lacking in professional experience. On the other hand, if you have been very active in college activities, don't get carried away. Be selective. Use this section to *enhance* your resume; don't let it *become* your resume. After you have listed these activities, etc., decide what descriptive title would best fit what you have listed.

TITLE _____

_____
_____
_____
_____
_____
_____
_____
_____
_____
_____
_____
_____
_____
_____

## INTERESTS

There are conflicting opinions as to whether it is advisable to include personal **interests** on your resume. R. Ernest Johnston, a career counselor, advises resume writers to use personal information about themselves and their interests because employers dislike hiring strangers. Another counselor, Cindy Elflein, on the other hand, lumps hobbies along with personal data as information that should not be included on a resume, stating that their inclusion is outdated and unprofessional. Steve Cohen and Paul de Oliveira, authors of *Getting to the Right Job*, advise us not to include hobbies and interests unless they are highly unusual or impressive and related directly to the job being applied for. They state, "It is highly unlikely that a fellow needlepointer is going to hire you on the basis of your handiwork" (p. 139).

This illustrates the point that in resume writing, as in everything else, you should get all the advice you can and then use common sense to make your own decisions. Just remember that the purpose of the resume is to present your qualifications in the best possible light and that an effective resume should be, among other things, *persuasive, concise,* and *focused*. With these thoughts in mind, it seems to me that Cohen and Oliveira's advice might be the best to follow. Include interests only if they are unusual, impressive, or relevant. Interests may give some substance to your resume if you have little experience and your resume looks meager. Interests might show something about you—that you are creative, or energetic, or enterprising—that would interest an employer. But if you can show such qualities in other ways, through work experience, activities, memberships, etc., or if your resume is fairly full, then my advice to you is not to include interests on your resume.

## REFERENCES

The last section of your resume focuses on **references**. This section identifies people with authority who know something about your work habits. This would include former employers, work supervisors, and teachers.

Before you use anyone's name as a reference, you should be sure that they will not mind writing a reference for you. You should also be sure that whomever you use as a reference feels comfortable writing a recommendation for you. It might be helpful for these people to know the kind of job for which you are applying so that they can write a recommendation that emphasizes those qualifications.

The reference section of most resumes merely says:

References available upon request.

Sometimes the names, addresses, and telephone numbers of references are listed at the bottom of a resume, but usually references are simply acknowledged as available. Listing references at the bottom of a resume takes up space that could be used to better advantage. None of the model resumes in this book list references on the resume.

Mary Ellen Guffey, author of *Essentials of Business Communication*, suggests that you do not even have to mention references on your resume because personnel directors do not need to be told that references will be made available on request. A couple of model resumes in this book follow this format and omit mention of references altogether.

If you include a note at the bottom of your resume that references are available or if you omit mention of references altogether, you need to prepare a reference sheet with the names, addresses, and telephone numbers of your references. You should bring this sheet with you to all interviews.

If you are registered with a university placement office, you probably have copies of transcripts, reference letters, etc., on file in the placement office. If this is your situation, you should have a statement like the following at the bottom of your resume:

Credentials available from
Ohio State University Placement Office
262 High Street
Columbus, OH 43201

# ACTIVITY 2-7

List three or four people who know something of your work habits and would be willing to provide a reference for you. Include their names, job titles, work telephone numbers, and work addresses.

_____

_____

_____

_____

_____

_____

_____

_____

## WHAT SHOULD NOT GO INTO YOUR RESUME

**Personal data** such as information about your age, height, weight, marital status, race, and religion should not be included on your resume. Although some of this information was once included, it has since been ruled that personal information may not legally be used in making decisions about employment. Employers may not ask for this information, and most employers would prefer not to see it on the resume.

## FORMAT AND LENGTH

There is no one correct format for your resume. Indeed, there are dozens of acceptable and effective styles. The format you choose is really a matter of personal preference. Remember that a resume must be attractive and readable; beyond that, it is up to you. The model resumes in this book have been cast in different ways so that you can get an idea of some of the more common formats.

Although the format you use is really a matter of personal choice, the type of resume—chronological, functional, or combined—depends on your specific situation. In Chapter 3, we will review the brief biographies of five job applicants. We will then consider the goal of each applicant and discover why each one decided to set up the resume as he or she did. We will also review examples of resumes that applicants revised and discover the reasons why the original drafts were considered inadequate.

## COPIES OF YOUR RESUME

When job hunting, you might prepare anywhere from one to several dozen copies of your resume. If you have access to a word processor, you can store your resume or resumes on a disk and print them as needed. If you do not have access to a word processor, you might want to consider having your resumes printed. Although that's the most expensive approach, it may be well worth the expense if you get the quality job you want.

You can even get your resume photocopied. If you're not a good typist, you can white out mistakes, and the Wite-Out ® will not show up on the photocopy. Often a good photocopy looks better than the original. If you photocopy your resume, you need to be sure that you do so on good quality paper.

# ACTIVITY 2-8

In this chapter, you have written down all of the elements that should appear on your resume. Now, go back through the chapter, gather up all your material, and put it together here as a rough draft.

HEADING

_____
_____
_____
_____

OBJECTIVE

_____
_____
_____

EDUCATION

_____
_____
_____
_____
_____

EXPERIENCE

_____
_____
_____
_____
_____
_____
_____
_____
_____
_____

"MISCELLANEOUS"

_____
_____
_____
_____
_____

When you have finished gathering this material, look back at your objective. Do your education and experience demonstrate the qualifications for the kind of work you wish to do? If the answer is no, you may want to rewrite your objective. Alternately, you may want to consider whether you have other qualifications that should be listed on your resume.

Look at the model resumes in Chapter 4 and Appendix A. Decide whether a chronological, functional, or combined resume would be best for you. Look at different formats and decide which you want to use. Finally, make a final draft of your resume. As you make your final draft, remember the qualities of a successful resume:

- Attractiveness
- Readability
- Persuasiveness
- Conciseness
- Focus

# SOFTWARE APPLICATION 3

The two applications in Chapter 2 will concentrate on the contents of your resume and will help you to prepare concise, focused, and persuasive information for the resumes that you prepare. Use this application, which provides you with practice in setting up and phrasing your resume in such a way as to emphasize your qualifications for a position you are interested in, to help you to ensure that each element on your resume reveals one of your qualifications.

# SOFTWARE APPLICATION 4

Use this application to create a database of notecards that you can use to prepare resumes and cover and follow-up letters.

# Using Hypothetical Cases to Find Your Format

## OBJECTIVES

**After you have studied this chapter, you should be able to:**

- Decide which experiences to include and which experiences to leave out of your resume.

- Recognize when your resume is sufficiently focused to help you get an interview.

- Determine whether a chronological, functional, or combined resume would be best for you.

- Set up two (or more) resumes for yourself, each aimed toward a different career.

- Critique your own resume and strengthen a weak or ineffective draft.

In this chapter, we'll use five hypothetical cases—brief biographies of fictitious job applicants—to find an effective format for your resume. Among these five individuals, you can probably find someone with a background or career goal somewhat similar to yours.

If you're able to find a similar job-seeking situation, don't simply take that individual's resume and use it as a model for your own. If there is more than one version of that resume, the first version may be an example of how *not* to set it up. Look at each applicant's background and resume. Note the reasons why he or she included or excluded information. When there is more than one draft, see if you can understand why the applicants decided to make the changes they did. After you have reviewed all of the resumes, choose the format you want to use for your own. Determine what you need to include and what you ought to leave out. Decide how you can state your qualifications in a way that will emphasize your strong points.

## MELODY MOONBEAM'S UPDATED RESUME

Melody Moonbeam has been working as a secretary in the law firm of Arthur, Wing, and Pinero for the past three years. This is her first job since graduating from Hathaway College in St. George, New Hampshire, with an A.S. degree in secretarial science. At Hathaway College, she was recording secretary of her sorority and she played intramural basketball. Melody worked part-time at Mc-Donald's during her last year of high school. She also worked part-time in college as a cashier in a supermarket. She is currently a member of Professional Secretaries International, attends the South Street Baptist Church regularly, and is interested in sewing, camping, and rock music.

Melody plans to get married in the spring. After her marriage, she will be living in Manchester, New Hampshire, so she is looking for a job as a secretary—preferably a legal secretary—in the Manchester area. Before beginning her job

**MELODY MOONBEAM**

14 Andover Street              Phone: (603) 555-2331
Somersworth, NH 03878

**Objective**

To obtain a position as a legal secretary

**Education**

199_            Hathaway College, St. George, NH:  A.S. degree in Secretarial Science, Major: Legal Secretary Program

Major Courses:

> Accounting II
> Business Law II
> Real Estate Law
> Machine Transcription
> Records Management
> Typing III
> Shorthand II

Milford High School, Milford, NH

Secretarial Skills:  Shorthand, 100 wpm
                     Typing, 60 wpm

**Work Experience**

July 199_—present                     Arthur, Wing, and Pinero
                                      Somersworth, NH

Legal Secretary.  Answer telephone and refer calls to appropriate person. Take dictation. Type letters.

199_–199_                             O'Hara's Superette
                                      St. George, NH

Checker.  Helped customers, restocked tobacco counter, ran cash register.

199_–199_                             McDonald's
                                      Milford, NH

Counter Person.  Took orders, served customers, ran cash register.

**Interests**

Sewing, Camping, Rock Music

**Memberships and Activities**

Sigma Sigma Sigma Sorority, Recording Secretary
Intramural Basketball
Professional Secretaries International
South Street Baptist Church

**References:**  Furnished upon request.

**Figure 3–1.** Melody Moonbeam's Updated Standard Resume

search, she updates her original standard (chronological) resume. The result is shown in Figure 3-1.

Melody visits the Placement Office at Hathaway College, where she learns that there are several secretarial openings in the Manchester area. Only one of them is in a law office. Melody shows the placement officer her updated resume, and he suggests several changes. Because Melody's objective limits her to working in a legal environment, her placement officer recommends that she make her objective more general.

Melody's work experience should be emphasized because it is her major qualification for a job. However, she needs to include more information regarding her specific duties as a legal secretary. The part-time jobs she had in high school and college need not be included on her resume because she has since had professional experience in the type of work she is seeking.

The education section of Melody's resume should include only her college background. Her high school courses and diploma should be left out.

The placement officer wonders about the college activities included under "Memberships and Activities." He finally decides that they should be left in because it has been only three years since Melody graduated from college. Melody's position in her sorority indicates that she was liked and respected by her sorority sisters. Her athletic activity shows that she can function as part of a team. Melody's interests and activities are neither unusual nor impressive; therefore, the placement officer suggests she leave them out.

Melody's revised resume is shown in Figure 3-2. This resume leaves out material that is not relevant or persuasive—such as her interests, her high school courses, and the part-time jobs she held while in school. It emphasizes her major qualification, which is her experience as a legal secretary, and highlights that experience by placing it before education and by providing more details about her duties as a legal secretary.

Melody's revised resume indicates that she puts her writing skills to work on her job by drafting routine letters. It also indicates that she is organized by stating that she coordinates the schedules of three junior partners. These activities suggest that Melody is able to establish priorities and work with people as well as work independently. In addition, she does monthly billing for her employer and knows how to operate a word processor. All of these activities indicate that she has the specific qualifications required for most secretarial positions.

Melody's revised resume is also a little more readable. Her format is almost exactly the same as it was in her first draft. The only major difference is that the headings are now capitalized, making it easier to see at a glance what is in each section.

# ACTIVITY 3-1

Why did Melody Moonbeam decide to leave the list of her college courses out of the second draft of her resume?

_____

_____

_____

What does the second draft of Melody's resume have that the first draft doesn't?

_____

_____

_____

**MELODY MOONBEAM**

14 Andover Street                                    Phone: (603) 555-2331
Somersworth, NH 03878

**OBJECTIVE**

To obtain a position as a legal secretary

**WORK EXPERIENCE**

July 199_—present                        Arthur, Wing, and Pinero
                                         Somersworth, NH

Legal Secretary.

Answer telephone and refer calls to appropriate person
Take dictation at 100 wpm
Type letters
Draft and type routine correspondence
Send out monthly bills
Use IBM-PC with Word-Star to prepare legal documents
Order office supplies
Route mail to appropriate persons
Coordinate schedules of three junior partners

**EDUCATION**

199_          Hathaway College, St. George, NH:  A.S. degree in Secretarial Science

             Secretarial Skills:      Shorthand, 100 wpm
                                       Typing, 60 wpm

**MEMBERSHIPS AND ACTIVITIES**

Sigma Sigma Sigma Sorority, Recording Secretary
Intramural Basketball
Professional Secretaries International
South Street Baptist Church

**REFERENCES:** Furnished upon request.

**Figure 3–2.** Melody Moonbeam's Revised Standard Resume

## HARRY DEXTER'S STANDARD RESUME

Harry Dexter will graduate from Hathaway College in May with an associate degree in travel and tourism. At the college placement office, he learns about an entry-level opening as a travel consultant. Although Harry has no paid work experience in travel and tourism, he has worked part-time in the Campus Men's Shop for the past year.

The placement officer gives Harry a format to follow for filling out his resume and suggests that he show her a rough draft before he sends it out. The format is designed for both recent graduates and students about to graduate. Because these individuals are typically limited in professional experience, the format includes relevant courses in their field. This allows them to get more information into their resumes, which should not be less than a page. The first draft of Harry's standard resume is shown in Figure 3-3.

When the placement officer reads Harry's first draft, she sees that it needs to be more developed. The draft covers little more than half a page. To be persuasive, the resume has to go into more detail.

The placement officer immediately notes that Harry has listed only his home address. Since there are still several months of school before graduation, the placement officer suggests that Harry list both his home address and his school address. She also suggests that Harry include the phrase "Candidate for A.S. degree" under *Education*.

Under *Prior Work Experience*, his placement officer suggests that Harry include some of the specific duties of his job at the Campus Men's Shop as well as those in the internship that he served in the college's travel agency. Although this was not paid work, it was work experience. The placement officer recommends that Harry include a section on his resume that lists the places to which he has traveled because a travel agency would be interested in that information. Finally, she suggests that Harry include some of his extracurricular activities and/or memberships to show that he is an active individual with professional interests. Harry's revised resume is shown in Figure 3-4.

# ACTIVITY 3-2

Name three items on Harry Dexter's revised resume that are not found on his first draft.

_____

_____

_____

_____

## HANNAH PETERSEN'S FUNCTIONAL RESUME

Hannah Petersen is about to graduate from Wayne State University with a degree in English. She worked one summer selling advertising for a weekly newspaper, the *Adrian Advertiser*. She also did some writing for the paper. For the past two years, she has been a reporter for the university newspaper. In high school, she was editor of her yearbook.

Hannah enjoyed working at the *Advertiser*, so she decides that she would like to go into journalism. Because her experience in this field is minimal, and her degree will be in English, not journalism, she decides to write a functional resume. With a functional resume she can put her experiences and extracurricular activities into skill clusters that will demonstrate her ability to work in an entry-level position in journalism. Her functional resume is shown in Figure 3-5.

HARRY DEXTER
RFD #1, Box 214
Saco, ME 04072
(207) 555-3441


**JOB OBJECTIVE**

To obtain a position as a travel consultant


**EDUCATION**

Hathaway College, St. George, NH, Major: Travel and Tourism 199_ to present


**RELEVANT MANAGEMENT AND TRAVEL COURSES**

Business Organization
Administrative Management
Principles of Marketing
Promotion Management

Reservations & Ticketing
Domestic Travel/Geography
Convention Management
International Travel/Geography
Travel & Tourism Management
Travel Agency Operation
Automated Airline Practicum


**PRIOR WORK EXPERIENCE**

Sept. 199_          Sales, Clerk, Campus Men's Store
present               St. George, NH


**REFERENCES**

Available upon request

**Figure 3–3.** First Draft of Harry's Standard Resume

**HARRY DEXTER**

PERMANENT ADDRESS                          PRESENT ADDRESS
RFD #1, Box 214                            Neville Hall
Saco, ME 04072                            Hathaway College
(207) 555-3441                            St. George, NH 03033
(after June 1, 199_)                      (until May 31, 199_)

**JOB OBJECTIVE**

To obtain a position as a travel consultant

**EDUCATION**

Candidate for A.S. degree in Travel & Tourism
Hathaway College, St. George, NH, 199_ to present

**RELEVANT MANAGEMENT AND TRAVEL COURSES**

Business Organization          Reservations & Ticketing
Administrative Management      Domestic Travel/Geography
Principles of Marketing        Convention Management
Promotion Management           International Travel/Geography
                               Travel & Tourism Management
                               Travel Agency Operation
                               Automated Airline Practicum

**PRIOR WORK EXPERIENCE**

Feb.–Mar.      Intern, Northern New England Travel Agency,
199_           Hathaway College
                    Sold travel packages
                    Made reservations and sold
                         airline tickets on a computer
                    Helped customers plan travel

Sept. 199_–    Sales, Clerk, Campus Men's Store
present        St. George, NH
                    Helped customers select clothes
                    Ran cash register
                    Developed ads for campus paper

**FOREIGN AND DOMESTIC TRAVEL**

Miami, FL                       Montreal, Canada
San Diego, CA                   London, England

**REFERENCES**

Available upon request

**Figure 3–4.** Harry Dexter's Revised Standard Resume

**HANNAH PETERSEN**
1457 Grove Street
Warren, MI 48091
(313) 555-7834

## OBJECTIVE

Seeking a position as editorial assistant or reporter.

## SKILLS, EXPERIENCE, AND ACCOMPLISHMENTS

—Writing/Editing—Staff Writer for independent weekly newspaper, reporter for college newspaper, editor of high school yearbook.

—Reviewer—Wrote movie reviews for college newspaper.

—Freelance Writing—Poetry published in campus literary magazine and little magazines. Articles accepted for publication in two national magazines.

—Public Relations—Public relations head for sorority. Wrote newsletter for sorority alumnae.

—Advertising Sales—Sold advertising space for weekly newspaper and for college newspaper.

—Organization Skills—Set up campus writers' network.

## EDUCATION

Candidate for B.A. degree, English, Wayne State University, Detroit, MI, June 199_.

## HONORS AND ACTIVITIES

Dean's List. Wayne State University, every semester.
Corresponding Secretary, Beta Sigma Rho Sorority.
Member, Wayne State Writer's Network.
National Honor Society, Warren High School.

## REFERENCES

Furnished upon request.

**Figure 3–5.** Hannah Petersen's Functional Resume

# ACTIVITY 3-3

Hannah Petersen has had several summer jobs since she has been in college. Besides selling advertising for a weekly newspaper, she worked as a clerk-typist one summer and as a camp counselor another summer. She could have written a chronological resume listing these jobs under the Experience section of her resume. Why is the functional resume more likely to help her get a job in journalism?

_____

_____

_____

_____

## BRUCE CHANG'S COMBINED RESUME

Bruce has had a highly successful career as a real estate broker for the past 20 years. Before working in real estate, he spent a few years in the advertising department of a small regional business magazine.

Despite Bruce's success in real estate, he is dissatisfied with his present job and is considering a career change. He wants to do something that will have more of a social impact. Because his teenage son, Terry, has cerebral palsy, Bruce has read a lot about CP and has also been very active in a group of parents of handicapped children. His group has been successful in several projects, including getting a wheelchair ramp built in their public library and getting some improvements in the special education program in their local school system.

Bruce takes an evening course in social welfare at a nearby college. Before the course is over, he decides that he wants to be a social worker. Bruce has been sufficiently successful in the real estate business to have made some good financial investments, so he can afford the cut in pay that would result from changing careers. He learns that there is an opening for a social worker at the local cerebral palsy center and wants to apply for the job.

It seems to Bruce that a combined resume will best serve his purpose because his work experience is very different from the kind of work he is applying for. A **combined resume** lists qualifications in skill clusters like those on a functional resume. It also contains a chronological record of work experience. This type of resume will enable him to demonstrate that even though he works in a different field, he has the skills required for this new career. At the same time, he can show that he has had a successful career in business.

Before he begins to work on the resume itself, Bruce draws up a list of competencies required for social work. From his reading, his volunteer work, and the course he has taken in social welfare, he knows that the job requirements will include compassion, organizational ability, knowledge of social agencies and resources, writing ability, and skill in interpersonal communication—particularly on a one-to-one basis.

On Bruce's combined resume he tries to demonstrate that, despite his lack of professional experience, he has the qualifications for the position of social worker. (See Figure 3-6.)

Bruce also realizes that he may not have even the minimal qualifications for the position as a social worker at the Cerebral Palsy Center. He decides that if he doesn't get the job, he will look for real estate work with another agency and draws up a second resume geared toward real estate. (See Figure 3-7.)

In this second resume, Bruce leaves out references to courses in social welfare. Instead, he includes real estate courses he has taken. He also lists some of his special achievements in real estate. Bruce was not going to list his volunteer activities because they do not relate directly to real estate. On consideration, though, he decides to list these activities because they will present opportunities to make contacts with people interested in social welfare, and these contacts might eventually lead to business for him.

**Bruce Chang**
143 Elm Street
Webster Groves, MO 63119
(314) 555-2123

**JOB OBJECTIVE:**          To be a social worker at the St. Louis Cerebral Palsy Center

## INTERPERSONAL COMMUNICATION

*Worked with individuals to help them buy homes and secure mortgages.
*Talked with principal of Webster Groves Junior High School to try to work out some of the problems in the special education program.
*Have encouraged my son to aim high and achieve all he can despite his handicap.

## ORGANIZATION/IMPLEMENTATION

*Worked with Handicapped Access Committee to get a wheel chair ramp for the Webster Groves Public Library.
*Organized a committee to secure improvements in the Webster Groves Junior High School special education program.

## WRITING

*Have written hundreds of letters in the real estate business.
*Wrote letters to special education departments in other school systems to gather information about their programs.

## EXPERIENCE

*Real Estate Broker, Webster Realty, Webster Groves, MO 1976–present.
*Advertising Director, *Ozark Profiles*, Osage Beach, MO 1973–1976.

## EDUCATION

Introduction to Social Welfare, Webster College, currently enrolled.
B.A., Business Administration, St. Louis University, 1973.

## ACTIVITIES AND MEMBERSHIPS

*Chair, Handicapped Access Committee
*Member, Special Education Committee, PTA
*Missouri Real Estate Association

**Figure 3–6.** Bruce Chang's Combined Resume

## Bruce Chang
143 Elm Street
Webster Groves, MO 63119
(314) 555-2123

## JOB OBJECTIVE

Seeking a position as a real estate broker

## PROFESSIONAL SALES EXPERIENCE

* Webster Realty.  Twenty years experience as a real estate broker.
* Member of the Million Dollar Club twelve of the last twenty years.
* Top salesperson at Webster Realty, 1987, 1989, and 1991.
* Advertising Director, *Ozark Profiles*, three years. Increased advertising revenue by 50% in the three-year period.

## PROFESSIONAL EDUCATION

* B.A. Business Administration, St. Louis University, 1973.
* Missouri Real Estate Sales Training Course.
* Real Estate Law, LaClede College
* Real Estate Practices, LaClede College
* Real Estate Appraisal, LaClede College
* Advanced Real Estate Sales Course, Missouri Real Estate Association

## MEMBERSHIPS AND ACTIVITIES

Missouri Real Estate Association
Missouri Multiple Listing Service
Greater St. Louis Business Association
Chair, Handicapped Access Committee
Special Education Committee, PTA

## REFERENCES

Available upon request

**Figure 3–7.** Bruce Chang's Real Estate Resume

# ACTIVITY 3-4

If Bruce Chang needs a resume for a job in real estate, why doesn't he just take the resume he wrote for the job at the Cerebral Palsy Center and change the objective?

_____

_____

_____

## HATTIE MAYBERRY'S REVISED RESUME

After Hattie was married in 1973, she stayed home to take care of the house and raise a family. When her marriage broke up, she went back to school to get a license as a nurse's aide. After graduation, Hattie went to work at the Manhattan Home for the Aged in Manhattan, Kansas, where she has been for three years.

Now Hattie is ready to make a change and calls an employment agency that specializes in placements in the health care professions. The employment counselor tells Hattie to come in and bring a resume with her. (See Figure 3-8.)

The employment counselor spots a number of problems with Hattie's resume. First, her jobs are not listed in reverse chronological order. The list of jobs should start with her current or most recent employment and then work back in time.

Second, there is a 17-year gap in Hattie's employment. Because her jobs from 1970–1973 are not related to the kind of work she is now qualified to do, there is no reason to list them, nor is there any advantage in listing her reasons for leaving them. On the other hand, she should list some of her duties and responsibilities on her certified nurse's aide job.

Third, her employment counselor sees that there is no need for Hattie to list her high school education on her resume because she has post-secondary training. She should list her internship, however, and include some of the high points of her training because she has only three years of experience.

Fourth, a Personal section is no longer included on a resume. Date of birth, marital status, etc., are not legally considered in making decisions about hiring, and employers cannot ask questions about these matters.

Fifth, it is not "wrong" to include references on the bottom of a resume, but Hattie's references are not very impressive. Furthermore, it is more effective to use this space to show something such as duties performed on the job or specific skills related to the job. These would emphasize Hattie's qualifications for the position. Hattie's neighbor doesn't know what kind of a worker she is, and although her co-worker at the Manhattan Home for the Aged probably knows something about Hattie's work, it would be more impressive to list work supervisors or former teachers at Eastern Kansas VTI as references. Generally, it's best to have a reference sheet—a separate paper with names, titles, business phones, and addresses of three or four people who are willing to serve as references if asked for. In Hattie's case, it is not necessary because she has a placement folder at Eastern Kansas VTI.

Hattie's employment counselor gives her some suggestions about ways she might revise her resume. Her revised resume, based on these suggestions, is shown in Figure 3-9.

```
Hattie Mayberry
745 O'Fallon Street, Apt. 41
Manhattan, KS 66506
(913) 555-4126

                          EMPLOYMENT

1970–1971          Store clerk, part-time, McCrory's
                   Osage city, KS
                   Reason for leaving:  To accept position at Topeka
                   City Hall

1971–1973          Office Clerk, City Hall, Topeka, KS
                   Reason for leaving:  To get married

1990–Present       Certified Nurse's Aide, Manhattan Home for the
                   Aged, Manhattan, KS

                          EDUCATION

1967–1971          Osage City High School

1989–1990          Eastern Kansas Vocational Technical Institute,
                   Topeka, KS
                   Certified Nurse's Aide diploma

                          PERSONAL

Born:              5/14/53. Divorced; one child; health: good
Membership:        Grace Baptist Church
Hobbies:           Sewing, gardening, gourmet cooking

                          REFERENCES

Harold L. Grangely                 Kimberly Curtis
neighbor                           co-worker
745 O'Fallon St., Apt. 24          329 Wayside Drive
Manhattan, KS 66506                Manhattan, KS 66506
(913) 555-2367                     (913) 555-2121
```

**Figure 3–8.** Hattie Mayberry's Original Resume

# ACTIVITY 3-5

Name five problems with the first draft of Hattie Mayberry's resume.

_____

_____

_____

_____

_____

HATTIE MAYBERRY
745 O'Fallon Street, Apt. 41
Manhattan, KS 66506
(913) 555-4126

## OBJECTIVE

Seeking a position as a certified nurse's aide in a nursing home.

## EMPLOYMENT

1990–present      Certified Nurse's Aide, Manhattan Home for the Aged, Manhattan, KS

Cases include victims of stroke, burns, accidents, and Alzheimer's disease

Duties include giving bed baths, changing bandages, keeping patient charts, and helping patients with meals

Help patients by reading to them, writing letters, taking them for walks, and organizing other recreational activities.

## EDUCATION

Eastern Kansas Vocational Technical Institute, Topeka, KS
Certified Nurse's Aide diploma, 1990

One-year course included patient care, emergency techniques, medication, geriatrics

Nine-week internship at Topeka General Hospital included training in patient care, report writing, and geriatrics.

## MEMBERSHIPS

Grace Baptist Church

## REFERENCES

Placement Office
Eastern Kansas Vo-Tech Institute
937 Broad Street
Topeka, KS 66603
(913) 555-0221

**Figure 3–9.** Hattie Mayberry's Revised Resume

## DIANA VELEZ'S CHRONOLOGICAL RESUME

Diana Velez ran her own interior decorating business for almost 10 years before deciding it was time to make a change. She had begun working immediately after high school and eventually started her own business. Now she wanted to return to college and begin a new career.

After completing her A.S degree, Diana prepares the resume shown in Figure 3-10. Although there are gaps in her employment history, Diana has decided to use a standard resume. She starts with her current job, then describes her previous job, and so on. The chronological resume works well for her because it presents a clear picture of her job history and shows increasing responsibility. An employer would probably assume that Diana was raising children during the gaps in her employment. Given the high levels of responsibility that she has attained in her career, Diana's resume is impressive. The first job listed, the office manager position, is actually a low-level job where she worked part-time during her last year of college. She was the only one in the office, but her title was office manager, and she did do the things that are listed on her resume.

Using this resume, Diana Velez got exactly the kind of job she was looking for on her first interview.

# ACTIVITY 3-6

Diana Velez could say that she is responsible and has leadership qualities. But she doesn't have to use these empty adjectives because there are specific examples of each of these on her resume. List three experiences that support each of these qualifications.

_____

_____

_____

_____

_____

_____

# ACTIVITY 3-7

At the end of Chapter 2, you were asked to write a rough draft of your resume. That draft was geared toward a particular career. Think of a second career or a related career for which you might have some qualifications. For example, you might consider the management or administrative area of a technical career or sales in relation to your field. You might think about an entry-level job in a different field. Be creative! Be adventurous! The only requirement for this activity is that you choose a field for which you would have minimum qualifications for at least an entry-level position.

Once you have decided on a field, determine what kind of resume would be best to get you into that field—standard (chronological), functional, or combined. After you decide, write a draft of the resume for your second career choice.

# SOFTWARE APPLICATION 5

Use this application, which explores the advantages and disadvantages of presenting information in *functional*, *chronological*, and *combination* formats, to produce attractive, easy-to-read resumes based on content you created for yourself in previous activities.

DIANA VELEZ
215 Wisteria Drive
Westbrook, ME 04092
(207) 555-1234

OBJECTIVE

To obtain a challenging position in the field of accounting

EDUCATION

Candidate for A.S. degree in Accounting, Andover College, May 199_

EXPERIENCE

Office Manager, Smith and Jones, Portland, ME (199_—present)
      * Run office, pay all bills
      * Order all supplies for lab and office
      * Keep the books and do the quarterly reports

Owner, Harris' Custom Designs, Westbrook, ME (1981–1991)
      * Supervised five employees in construction and installation of draperies
      * Worked with designers and private clients
      * Measured and estimated jobs
      * Kept books, did payroll, made quarterly reports

Front-End Supervisor, Bradlee's, Westbrook, ME (1973–1976)
      * Supervised cashiers and service desk
      * Did all scheduling
      * Trained all new employees

Bookkeeper, Consumers Gas, Portland, ME (1964–1967 and 1977–1979)
      * Responsible for billing, accounts receivable, accounts payable
      * Scheduled deliveries of bottled gas
      * Sold appliances and fire and safety equipment from sales floor

AWARDS AND ACTIVITIES

President, Andover College Student Senate, 199_
Who's Who Among American Junior College Students, 199_
Dean's List, Andover College, all four semesters
Member American Business Women's Association

**Figure 3–10.** Diana Velez's Standard Resume

CHAPTER

4

# Developing an Effective Cover Letter

**OBJECTIVES**

**After you have studied this chapter, you should be able to:**

- Distinguish between a direct pattern and a persuasive cover letter.

- Differentiate between an invited and a prospecting cover letter.

- Write a direct pattern cover letter that is short and to the point.

- Write a prospecting and an invited cover letter.

- Write a persuasive cover letter that gains attention, demonstrates capability, and calls for action.

- Explain why sending out "snow storm" letters is not an effective means of getting a job interview.

- Find information about a company you are interested in working for.

- Write a cover letter that enhances your resume.

- Write cover letters in a natural, conversational style.

Although the typical job seeker will usually use many copies of a single resume when applying for different jobs, he or she will write an individual cover letter to go with that resume each time it is sent out.

Although the basic purpose of a **cover letter** is to accompany a resume, your cover letter can do a lot more. It can enhance and support your resume; it can provide extra details on crucial points; it can explain things in a way that your resume cannot; and it can help to persuade an employer that you are a candidate who should be interviewed.

To restate what was written about resumes in Chapter 1, a good cover letter will not get you a job for which you are not qualified, nor will it give you an edge over someone with better qualifications. It will, however, give you an advantage over someone with roughly the same qualifications as yours. This chapter will focus on the different types of cover letters available to you, and then discuss some of the important elements to remember when you write your next cover letter.

## TYPES OF COVER LETTERS

There are two types of cover letters: *direct pattern* and *persuasive*. Most people write direct pattern cover letters, and in most situations, they are adequate. In a highly competitive situation, however, the persuasive letter can make the difference between being interviewed and not being interviewed. Cover letters can also be classified as *invited* or *prospecting*. An invited cover letter is one that responds to some kind of job notice, whereas a prospecting cover letter goes to a company or companies where job openings may or may not exist. Prospecting and invited cover letters may be either direct pattern or persuasive.

When jobs are scarce, there is always more competition for available jobs. Even when there are many jobs, however, there is always competition for the best of them. Enclosing an effective cover letter with your resume is one way to put your best foot forward when striving for the job you want.

## DIRECT PATTERN COVER LETTERS

A **direct pattern cover letter** is one that says, "Here is my resume; I'm interested in the job opening that you advertised." It is brief and to the point. The first paragraph declares that you are applying for a specific position, and explains where you learned of the opening.

The second paragraph states that your resume is enclosed and points out in very general terms your major qualifications for the job. For example, you might explain where you got your degree and what your major was. You might briefly discuss related work experience.

The final paragraph requests an interview and provides a telephone number where you can be reached.

A typical pattern cover letter from Chapter 3, Melody Moonbeam, is shown in Figure 4-1. Although there is nothing wrong with such a letter, the letter by itself will not open any doors. There is nothing in this letter that is not already on the resume. If the firm of Shaw, Joyce and O'Casey needs a legal secretary with Melody's qualifications, they will probably interview her. But if they have to make a choice about whom to interview, and someone with similar qualifications writes a persuasive cover letter, they will be more likely to interview that person.

# ACTIVITY 4-1

Find a want ad for a job that interests you. Write a direct pattern cover letter applying for that job. In the first paragraph, name the job that interests you and state where you learned of the opening. In the second paragraph, state your major qualifications. In the third and final paragraph, request a job interview.

## PERSUASIVE COVER LETTERS

The purpose of a **persuasive cover letter** is to enhance the resume in such a way as to persuade the reader the you have the qualifications required for the job. On the surface, a persuasive cover letter might seem to be very much like a direct pattern letter, except that it is longer. That similarity, however, is indeed superficial.

A persuasive cover letter is more likely to help you get an interview in a competitive job market. A direct pattern cover letter simply says, "Here's my resume. Please consider me for your job opening." A persuasive cover letter, however, gives *reasons* why an employer should give serious consideration to your application and follows the same organizational pattern as a sales letter. It captures the reader's attention by showing what you can do for him or her. Next, it presents persuasive details about your qualifications. This type of cover letter requests an interview only after it has provided good reasons for an employer to

14 Andover Street
Somersworth, NH 03878
April 21, 199_

Ms. Molly Bloom
Shaw, Joyce and O'Casey
782 Elm Street
Manchester, NH 03063

Dear Ms. Bloom:

I would like to apply for the position of legal secretary that was advertised through the Placement Office of Hathaway College.

I graduated from Hathaway College in 1986 with an AS degree in secretarial science. Since graduation I have been working for the law firm of Arthur, Wing and Pinero in Somersworth. At Arthur, Wing and Pinero I do routine typing and prepare legal documents on an IBM-PC. My resume is enclosed.

I will be happy to come to Manchester for an interview at any mutually convenient time. If my qualifications are the ones you are looking for, please call me at (603) 555-4332.

Sincerely,

*Melody Moonbeam*

Melody Moonbeam

Encl.

**Figure 4–1.** Melody Moonbeam's Direct Pattern Cover Letter

consider you for a job. A persuasive cover letter can make your application stand out in a crowd.

There are three steps to writing a persuasive cover letter:

- Gain attention
- Demonstrate capability
- Call for action

In Figure 4-2 you will see another cover letter from Melody Moonbeam. This one is a persuasive rather than direct pattern letter. As you look at this letter, you will see how it gains attention, demonstrates capability, and calls for action.

**Gain Attention.** You gain the attention of a busy employer by suggesting that you can do something for that individual. You might gain attention merely by clearly stating that you are interested in filling a vacancy that exists in that person's organization. The opening of this type of letter might be the same as the opening for a direct pattern cover letter.

14 Andover Street
Somersworth NH 03878
March 28, 199_

MS. FRANCIS GLASS
GARDNER, SALINGER AND DONLEAVY
213 BEDFORD STREET
MANCHESTER NH 03063

Dear Ms. Glass:

The placement office at Hathaway College told me that the firm of Gardner, Salinger and Donleavy has a secretarial opening for which I might be qualified. I could bring to Gardner, Salinger and Donleavy a sense of responsibility as well as excellent secretarial, organizational, and writing skills.

The firm of Arthur, Wing and Pinero considered me sufficiently responsible that, after I had worked there for six months, I was given the task of training new secretaries in our office procedures. In addition, one of my duties at Arthur, Wing and Pinero was to draft and type routine letters. I was frequently chosen to take minutes of meetings because of my skill in shorthand. Coordinating the schedules of three junior partners as well as managing my own work flow efficiently required a great deal of organizational ability. This was particularly true when the office was busy, which it frequently was.

I would welcome an opportunity to discuss my qualifications for this position with you. I will be calling you within the next week to see if we can set up an appointment at a mutually convenient time.

Sincerely,

*Melody Moonbeam*

Melody Moonbeam

Enclosure

**Figure 4–2.** Melody Moonbeam's Persuasive Cover Letter

There are other elements, however, that can be included in the opening of a persuasive cover letter. For example, you might detail several of your major qualifications for the job in your first paragraph. If the letter were opened this way, then you would go on in your second paragraph to provide evidence that you possess the qualifications that you have claimed. For example, if you state in your opening paragraph that you are well-organized, you need to show in your second paragraph what you have done that required organizational skill.

Another way to catch an employer's attention is to write a **personalized cover letter** to show that you know something about him or the company for which he is working (and for which you would like to work). This requires some research, of course, but if you want go get the best job possible, you need to do the upfront work.

In the opening of her cover letter in Figure 4-2, Melody not only states that she is applying for a job, she gives her major qualifications. The middle part of her letter then offers evidence of those qualifications. The evidence of her organizational ability is the statement that she was able to coordinate the schedules of three junior partners and at the same time manage her own work flow efficiently. Notice that the personal pronoun "I" is used minimally in this paragraph.

**Demonstrate Capability.** This is the part of the cover letter that is most different from the direct pattern letter. It is here that most of the persuasion takes place. Consequently, the middle part of this letter is much longer than the middle part of the direct pattern letter. Instead of one short paragraph, there will be a well-developed paragraph or even several paragraphs.

In this section of your letter, you state your major qualifications for the position. However, instead of merely referring to past degrees, job titles, and duties, you zero in on the specific requirements of the job for which you are applying. If the job requires organizational ability, for example, you refer to things you have done that required organizational ability.

It is important here to state your capabilities without sounding boastful. The way to do this is to use specific rather than general statements. For example, if you write something like this:

> I have impressive leadership and organizational ability

most employers will not find such a statement convincing. A more effective way to communicate this is to give specific examples of accomplishments that demonstrate your leadership and organizational ability:

> After working for the Big Apple store for a little over a month, I was promoted to assistant manager and two months later to manager. Part of my responsibility was to organize work schedules. This was not an easy task because we were chronically short-handed. However, my store consistently received high ratings from supervisors for cleanliness, inventory control, and employee morale.

Melody presented her job qualifications well in her letter partly by using the first person singular as little as possible. Also, rather than writing, "I am well-organized," or "I have good writing skills," she showed what she had done to demonstrate those capabilities. In addition, she indicated how other people in her company confirmed those qualities. If she didn't write well, someone would send a letter back asking her to do it over. If she were not considered responsible, she would not have been chosen to train new secretaries in office procedures at Gardner, Salinger and Donleavy.

**Call for Action.** This part of the letter is just the same as the last part of the direct pattern cover letter. It requests an interview and provides a telephone number where you can be reached. The only difference is that in the persuasive letter, you attempt to convince the employer to set up an interview by demonstrating your qualifications.

# ACTIVITY 4-2

Write a cover letter applying for one of the jobs in the classified ads on pages 10–15 or bring in an actual want ad from the newspaper. In your first paragraph, state the job for which you are applying. For the purpose of this application, assume that the advertisement appeared in last Sunday's issue of your local paper.

Read between the lines in the advertisement to discover the major requirements for the position. In the middle part of your letter, demonstrate your qualifications for the position. Make specific rather than general statements so that your letter will be persuasive and won't sound boastful. In your final paragraph, ask confidently for an interview or state that you will call to see if you can set up an interview.

## INVITED AND PROSPECTING COVER LETTERS

Cover letters, sometimes called application letters, may also be prospecting or invited. An **invited cover letter** comes in response to an invitation for individuals to apply for a specific job opening. An advertisement in the newspaper is an example of such an invitation. A notice to a public, private, or college placement agency is also an example of an invitation as are notices of openings placed in professional journals.

A **prospecting cover letter** is one that is sent when you do not know whether an employer has an opening. You might wonder why you would ever go to all the trouble of applying for a job when you don't even know if a job exists. The answer is that many jobs are filled this way. Most jobs are never advertised. Employers simply depend on incoming applications from which they can fill the openings that occur in the company.

The major difference between prospecting and invited cover letters is that with the invited application, you usually know exactly what the job requirements are, whereas with the prospecting application you have to use your best judgment as to what the job requirements might be.

You can clearly see the difference between invited and prospecting cover letters if you look at the two letters written by Hannah Petersen. The first letter, shown in Figure 4-3, is an invited application; it is a response to an advertisement that appeared in the *Detroit News*. Here is the ad to which Hannah responded.

> Assistant Editor—to be trained to become editor of a weekly paper. Must be flexible. Reporting, photography and copy editing involved. Send resume and clips.

When we looked at this ad near the beginning of the book, we read between the lines and determined that the successful candidate would need a thorough knowledge of the English language, management skills, responsibility, and initiative.

Hannah wonders whether she should apply for this job. She is not only young, but she has relatively little experience, having worked only one summer in a paid newspaper job. However, she is bright and confident. The ad does not state that experience is required, so the training period could be fairly extensive. Possibly the editor is also the publisher; he may want to retire in a couple of years and has decided to train a good replacement for himself. Hannah decides to go ahead and send in her resume and cover letter.

Hannah knows that there will be qualified applicants who have more experience than she has, so she emphasizes other things, including her sense of responsibility and her intelligence. Instead of calling herself intelligent, however, she says she is a quick learner. She also points out that although her experience is limited, it is also broad because she has been involved in many aspects of journalism.

While she is sending out applications, Hannah also decides to send a resume and a prospecting cover letter to *The Detroit Free Press*. Her prospecting letter is shown in Figure 4-4. Hannah doesn't know whether the paper has an opening, but she assumes that a large city newspaper is bound to have positions to fill from time to time. She doesn't have any specific requirements to guide her, but she knows that writing ability and experience are going to be very important. She

1467 Grove St.
Warren, MI 48091

April 27, 199_

Mr. Frank Craig
Editor
Defiance Crescent-News
Defiance, OH 43512

Dear Mr. Craig:

I am writing in response to the advertisement in *The Detroit News* for an assistant editor for the *Defiance Crescent News*. You will find me to be a responsible person who picks things up very quickly. In my short career I have worked at every phase of journalism from advertising sales to photography to writing and editing.

From high school onward I have shown a deep sense of responsibility. Partly because of this sense of responsibility, my grades in school have always been good. I was in the National Honor Society in high school and on the Dean's List in college. My work with the high school yearbook began during my sophomore year. In my senior year the yearbook advisor chose me to be editor. I have always been one who has seen what needs to be done and have gone ahead and done it. My setting up of a campus writers' network at Wayne State University is an example of this.

Whenever a task has been given to me, I have learned very quickly how to do it. During the summer of 1988 when I was working for the *Adrian Advertiser*, the person who had been teaching me about advertising sales was hospitalized just a few days after I started on the job. I picked up the job with minimal supervision; the editor didn't have much time to work with me. Before the summer was over, advertising sales had increased nearly 10% over the same period the previous year.

Between working on my high school yearbook, the *Wayne Stater*, and the *Adrian Advertiser*, I have worked in virtually every phase of journalism. I sold advertising, took pictures occasionally, and wrote articles for both the *Wayne Stater* and the *Adrian Advertiser*. I edited copy for my high school yearbook, the *Forum*. My resume and clips are enclosed.

I will give your office a call sometime during the next week to see if we can set up an appointment to talk about my qualifications for the position of assistant editor of the *Defiance Crescent News*.

Sincerely,

Hannah Petersen

Hannah Petersen

Encl.

**Figure 4–3.** Hannah Petersen's Invited Cover Letter

1467 Grove St.
Warren, MI 48091

May 4, 199_

Ms. Shirley Finch
Human Resources Director
The Detroit Free Press
615 West Lafayette
Detroit, MI 48239

Dear Ms. Finch:

Is there an opening on the *Detroit Free Press* for a reporter with good writing skills, tenacity, and a strong sense of responsibility? I will be graduating from Wayne State University in a few weeks, and I would like to be considered for any opening that you might have.

As a staff writer for the *Adrian Advertiser* and a reporter for the *Wayne Stater*, I wrote over 150 articles and 150 reviews. During my last two years in college I wrote and edited a sorority newsletter that comes out three times a year.

I believe tenacity is an important attribute for a reporter. During the summer of 1988 when I was working for the *Adrian Advertiser*, the actress Margot Williams spent some time at a lake near Adrian. She definitely did not want to talk to reporters, but I kept going back until she granted me an interview.

In the activities in which I have engaged, I have always risen to positions of responsibility. At the *Adrian Advertiser*, for example, the person who was in charge of advertising sales was hospitalized a few days after I started on the job. I learned pretty much on my own how to do advertising sales and handled that responsibility along with my writing responsibilities through the summer. The editor of the *Adrian Advertiser* was sufficiently pleased with my work that he asked me to return after I graduated from college. As tempting as that offer was, I decided not to accept it because I wanted to broaden my experience by working for a big city newspaper, particularly a paper with the reputation and prestige of the *Detroit Free Press*.

I would welcome an opportunity to further discuss my qualifications with you. I will be calling you within the next week to see if I can set up an appointment with you.

Sincerely,

Hannah Petersen

Hannah Petersen

Encl.

**Figure 4–4.** Hannah Petersen's Prospecting Cover Letter

thinks that persistence, the willingness to stick to a story lead until she has dug up the facts, will be important. Responsibility will not be as important for a beginning reporter as it would be for an assistant editor training to become an editor, but she knows that responsibility is important on any job.

These are the qualities Hannah emphasizes in her cover letter. She also shows that she is responsible by explaining that she has been invited back to work on the *Adrian Advertiser*. She does not want to accept that offer, mostly because the pay is low, but that is not the reason she gives in her cover letter.

Hannah ends her letter as she did the letter that responded to the advertisement for an assistant editor—stating that she will give them a call. Some people might feel that it is a little pushy to do that rather than to request that the employer call her. There is nothing wrong with stating that she will call, however, particularly in a field such as reporting where aggressiveness is a desired quality.

Hannah addresses the letter to Shirley Finch, the Human Resources Director. Where did she get Shirley Finch's name? She called the newspaper and asked for it.

# ACTIVITY 4-3

Diane Velez, whose resume is shown in Figure 3-9, saw the following ad in her local newspaper:

> High Energy, Well-Organized Office Manager
> Accounts receivable/accounts payable, budgeting and planning, computer skills a must. Creative thinker, willing to take charge. Send resume to Florence Murphy.

Here is Diane's letter in response to this ad:

> Dear Ms. Murphy:
>
> Please consider me for the office manager position that was advertised in the *Portland Press Herald*. I can bring to this job the combination of high energy and good organization skills that you require.
>
> Owning a custom draper shop required a lot of organization as I coordinated the activities of the workshop and the on-site installations. Besides designing and managing the production and installation of custom draperies, I was often on the road doing estimates. It was not unusual for me to work 50 or even 60 hours a week.
>
> At Andover College, I have taken three computer courses. I am very comfortable with WordPerfect and Lotus 1-2-3, having used them extensively at Smith and Jones. My experience in accounts receivable and accounts payable goes back many years.
>
> If you are looking for a well-organized, high-energy, take-charge manager, a creative thinker with extensive experience in budgeting and planning, please give me a call at 854-1234.
>
> Sincerely,
> Diane Velez

While Diane is applying for the job that was advertised, she decides to send her resume to a large insurance company to apply for a job as office manager. Write a prospecting cover letter to this company for Diane. Here is their address:

> Blue Cross and Blue Shield of Maine
> 5 Gannett Drive
> South Portland, ME 04106

## "SNOW STORM" LETTERS

Some people seem to think that if you can send a resume and cover letter to one organization that may or may not have an opening in your field, you can just as easily write to *every* organization that employs people in your field. These letters are sometimes called **"snow storm" letters** because they seem almost to blanket the countryside like a snow storm.

Such letter campaigns are rarely effective. If you are going to write to 30 or 40 or 50 organizations, you are not likely to take the time to research each one. Although it is true that if you send out enough letters, one or two of them are likely to land where an opening exists; this does not necessarily mean that you will be offered the position. The position is more likely to be offered to someone who has researched an opening and personalized the cover letter.

## WRITING AN EFFECTIVE COVER LETTER

In order to write an effective cover letter, you need to know something about the company where you want to work. You also need your cover letter to enhance your resume. You do this by focusing in the cover letter on those skills that relate to a specific opening. Finally, you need to establish a writing style that will make you seem warm and human rather than stiff and pompous.

### LEARN SOMETHING ABOUT THE COMPANY AND THE INDIVIDUAL TO WHOM YOU ARE WRITING

When we reviewed the way a persuasive cover letter is set up, we said that this type of letter begins by gaining attention. One way to gain that attention is to let the employer know you are interested in filling an existing vacancy in the employer's organization. There are, however, other ways to gain attention and capture the reader's interest.

*"Basically, we're aiming at an audience of adventuresome, outdoor-oriented, upwardly mobile young males."*

Drawing by D. Reilly; © 1991 The New Yorker Magazine, Inc.

Two things that always interest people are their jobs and themselves. For this reason, a cover letter is more effective if it contains a reference to the employing organization or the individual who is to receive the letter.

Think of it from the point of view of the person receiving a cover letter. If you had to choose between two applicants, and one of them addressed the letter to you by name, spelled your name correctly, and showed some knowledge of your organization, whereas the other letter was simply addressed to "Dear Personnel Manager," which applicant would you interview?

It is not only that employers are more impressed by someone who knows something about them and the place they work; they are also impressed that the applicant has had enough interest and ambition to research the position. Furthermore, an applicant is likely to find things in his or her research that might help to tailor that application more effectively for a specific situation.

There are all sorts of ways to get the kind of information you need about an organization. If you're interested in working for a major corporation, you can and should go to the library and use *The Reader's Guide* or the *Business Index* to research that organization. You can also get information about trends in particular areas of business and about developments in individual companies by reading business magazines and the business section of news magazines and newspapers.

These sources of information can tell you which businesses are doing well and which ones are doing poorly. They can tell you about new developments in the market, new products, new companies, and new branches of old companies. These magazines and newspapers can also give you information about the people who are involved in these new developments in business.

If you are applying for a job with a local company or a local branch of a large company, newspapers, special newspaper supplements, and local business magazines can provide you with information that you can use as you prepare your application.

Most Sunday papers have a business section. Many daily papers focus once a week on personnel changes in local business, giving a thumbnail sketch of people who have been promoted or appointed to new positions. Often the individuals described in these sketches are the middle-management people who make many of the decisions about hiring.

From time to time, both daily and Sunday papers come out with special supplements that pertain to business. The *Portland Press Herald* in Portland, Maine, for example, has had three such special supplements in less than a month. One of these supplements dealt with careers and career education. A second supplement was prepared for public relations purposes by a bank that had recently been reorganized. It contained lot of information about projects that the bank was involved in, as well as information about individuals who worked in the bank, including department heads and branch managers. The third supplement, called "Business Profiles Review," contained nearly 100 brief profiles of small businesses in the area.

Besides newspapers, there are usually magazines devoted to local businesses. Among those published in Portland, Maine, *Business Digest* has several pages of brief sketches of people in business. One of these sketches in a recent issue of the magazine concerned someone who had just been named senior vice president of an investment firm. Another notice was about an individual who had just joined a company as a marketing assistant. In addition to these brief notices, the magazine takes an in-depth look at several local businesses each month.

Here is the way this type of information can help you draft a more effective cover letter. Harry Dexter read an article in a newspaper supplement about careers in travel and tourism. Later he read about a travel agency in "Business Profiles Review." He decided to put together information from these two sources and use this as an attention getter in a persuasive cover letter to the travel agency. His cover letter is shown in Figure 4-5.

RFD #1, Box 214
Saco, ME 04072

May 7, 199_

Ms. Holly Columbine
Marchand Travel Service
29 Coin Street
Portland ME 04101

Dear Ms. Columbine:

When I read an article about the growth of the travel and tourism business, I knew I had chosen the right career. Then when I read a profile of Marchand Travel Service in *Business Profiles*, I was sure of it. Like Marchand Travel and Service, I believe that attention to detail is a key to success, particularly in the travel business where there are so many little details that become crucial as a trip or tour progresses. This is one of the things I have learned in my education at Hathaway College.

The Hathaway College Travel and Tourism program offers a unique blend of classroom training and direct experience that prepares people for careers in the travel industry. At Hathaway College, I learned the reservation and ticketing system in the classroom. This knowledge was then applied in the direct experience of the Automated Airline Practicum where I learned how to use a computer to make reservations and sell airline tickets. The practicum was performed at Hathaway College's Northern New England Travel Agency. Northern New England Travel Agency is an operating agency. Students in the agency's practicum deal with actual customers who want to use the agency's services.

After taking courses in marketing and promotion, I worked in the travel agency doing direct sales and learning all aspects of the operation of a travel agency. Students in the practicum spend a total of ninety hours working in the travel agency.

Another direct experience that was part of my education included travel to San Diego and to London. In London, I studied for three weeks at the Pan American Academy. The Travel and Tourism program at Hathaway College included extensive reviews of airport codes and of domestic and international geography. With my classroom training and direct experience, I feel well-prepared to begin working as a travel consultant.

I will be receiving my degree in Travel and Tourism from Hathaway College in just a few weeks. I would welcome an opportunity to talk with you about my qualifications for a position at Marchand Travel Service. I will be calling you in the next week or two to see if we can set up an appointment at a mutually convenient time.

Sincerely,

*Harry Dexter*

Harry Dexter

Encl.

**Figure 4–5.** Harry Dexter's Persuasive Cover Letter

# ACTIVITY 4-4

Use the library or other sources to find five pieces of information about a particular company and/or a particular career. Look for information that could be used as attention getters in a cover later. Use this information to write an attention-getting opening for a cover letter.

## LET YOUR COVER LETTER ENHANCE YOUR RESUME

You can let your cover letter enhance your resume, emphasize your strengths, fill in gaps, and relate your qualifications more directly to the job. Because job applicants typically prepare a dozen or so copies of their resumes, your resume is probably going to be somewhat general so that it can fit several different jobs. Your cover letter can be more personalized, though.

For example, let's say that a job notice or an advertisement says, "Computer experience a plus." You don't have anything about computers on your resume because you've never worked with a computer on a job. However, you have worked as a volunteer on a political campaign inputting data on a computer. You didn't include it on your resume because you didn't consider the computer experience significant and you definitely don't consider it one of your strong points. This is the type of thing that can instead go into your cover letter to enhance your resume.

If you look at Bruce Chang's resume and cover letter in Figure 4-6a & b, you can see another example of the way a cover letter can be used to enhance a resume. Bruce's resume is geared toward one specific position: social worker at the St. Louis Cerebral Palsy Center. In many ways Bruce is a good candidate for this job, but he has two serious shortcomings—he has no experience and practically no training. He is only now taking his first course in social welfare. The center might even be a little suspicious of his volunteer work. Although he donated much of his time, everything Bruce did was directly related to his son's welfare. A social worker needs compassion but also must be able to view things objectively. The agency might wonder if Bruce will be able to view things dispassionately when he needs to.

Because Bruce is strongly aware of his deficiencies, he writes a cover letter that enhances his resume.

# ACTIVITY 4-5

In Activity 2-8 you were asked to write a rough draft of your resume, and in Activity 3-7 you were asked to write a rough draft of a resume for a second career or related career for which you had some qualifications. Now you will write cover letters to accompany these two resumes. In the first, let your cover letter enhance your resume, emphasize your strengths, fill in gaps, and relate your qualifications more directly to a job for which you would like to apply. In the second, write a cover letter that enhances your other resume. Focus on a deficiency that might otherwise inhibit an employer from hiring you for a position you seek.

## PAY ATTENTION TO YOUR WRITING STYLE

Notice that in the opening of Melody's letter to Gardner, Salinger and Donleavy in Figure 4-2, instead of saying that she is applying for an opening "which

<u>**Bruce Chang**</u>
143 Elm Street
Webster Groves, MO 63119
(314) 555-2123

**<u>JOB OBJECTIVE:</u>**      To be a social worker at the St. Louis Cerebral Palsy Center


**<u>INTERPERSONAL COMMUNICATION</u>**

*Worked with individuals to help them buy homes and secure mortgages.
*Talked with principal of Webster Groves Junior High School to try to work out some of the problems in the special education program.
*Have encouraged my son to aim high and achieve all he can despite his handicap.


**<u>ORGANIZATION/IMPLEMENTATION</u>**

*Worked with Handicapped Access Committee to get a wheel chair ramp for the Webster Groves Public Library.
*Organized a committee to secure improvements in the Webster Groves Junior High School special education program.


**<u>WRITING</u>**

*Have written hundreds of letters in the real estate business.
*Wrote letters to special education departments in other school systems to gather information about their programs.


**<u>EXPERIENCE</u>**

*Real Estate Broker, Webster Realty, Webster Groves, MO 1976–present.
*Advertising Director, *Ozark Profiles*, Osage Beach, MO 1973–1976.


**<u>EDUCATION</u>**

Introduction to Social Welfare, Webster College, currently enrolled.
B.A., Business Administration, St. Louis University, 1973.

**<u>ACTIVITIES AND MEMBERSHIPS</u>**

*Chair, Handicapped Access Committee
*Member, Special Education Committee, PTA
*Missouri Real Estate Association

**Figure 4–6a.** Bruce Chang's Resume and Cover Letter

143 Elm Street
Webster Groves MO 63119

November 17, 199_


Ms Maria Santiago
Director
St Louis Cerebral Palsy Center
1287 Kings Highway
St Louis Mo 63118

Dear Ms Santiago:

Victor Raddison, social worker at Webster Groves High School, told me that there was an opening for a social worker at the Cerebral Palsy Center. I would like to be considered for that position.

Although my resume may not show it, I have had a lot of experience doing social work. My son Terry, who is now 14, was born with cerebral palsy. In an effort to understand Terry's affliction and to help him become as independent as possible, I have done extensive research on the subject of cerebral palsy.

Since Terry's early childhood I have been active as a advocate for the handicapped. Committees that I have worked on or headed have been successful in bringing about changes that have made buildings, education, and recreational activities more accessible to handicapped people.

In 17 years of successful experience in the real estate business, I have demonstrated an ability to get things done and to work with people. I would like to begin using that successful experience to help people more directly as a social worker. I am now taking my first course in social work. I am planning to take two courses in social work next semester and continue taking courses until I can become a certified social worker.

If you are looking for someone who can bring mature judgment to a position, someone who is willing to give up a highly successful career so that he can help other people, please give me a call at 555-4552 during the day or at 555-2123 in the evening.

Sincerely,

Bruce Chang

Bruce Chang

Encl.

**Figure 4–6b.**

I might be qualified for," she applies for an opening "for which I might be qualified."

Melody's first statement ends a sentence with a preposition. There is nothing wrong with this in an informal situation. However, a job application letter is a little more formal than most business letters. You want to present yourself at your best. Just as you want to be sure that your clothes are just right when you go to an important business meeting, you need to be a little more careful about language on an application letter.

On the other hand, you don't want to be so formal that you come across as stiff and pompous. A hundred years ago, business letters were written in a very formal and flowery style. Some people still think that this unnatural style is required for business letters; it isn't. These people, who would never dream of using a century-old means of transportation or a 10-year-old clothing style, believe that they have to pepper their business letters with phrases that went out of conversation a century ago.

A cover letter, as any other business letter, should be written in a **natural style**, as though you are speaking. If you would not hand an envelope to someone and say, "Enclosed please find my resume," then it's also not a good idea to put that expression in your letter.

# ACTIVITY 4-6

Rewrite the following sentences in more up-to-date, free-flowing, natural language.

1. This writer has observed the work performance of Miss Pinkerton for the past three years.

   _____

   _____

   _____

2. In compliance with your request, enclosed please find two tickets to *The Phantom of the Ballet*.

   _____

   _____

   _____

3. Your letter is at hand and contents duly noted.

   _____

   _____

   _____

4. The material you ordered will be sent forthwith under separate cover.

   _____

   _____

   _____

5. As per your request, the *Handbook for Underachieving Wombats* is enclosed.

   _____

   _____

   _____

6. Permit me to say that our obligation in this matter has been completely fulfilled. _____

   _____

   _____

7. Please be advised that all applications are reviewed by the director personally.

_____

_____

_____

8. Due to the fact of my professional experience during that time frame, I gained insight into the process.

_____

_____

_____

9. This writer has utilized the utmost care in preparing this document.

_____

_____

_____

10. This is to inform you that you will soon be in receipt of the merchandise you ordered.

_____

_____

_____

# ACTIVITY 4-7

Rewrite the following letter in a more up-to-date, natural, and effective style.

Pursuant to your advertisement in _____ , I would appreciate it if you would take under consideration my application for a position as facilitator at your organization.

Enclosed please find my resume, which will show that from the beginning of my career, this writer has utilized the skills required for a facilitator. At this point in time, this writer is fully cognizant of the difficulties inherent in such a position, but this writer remains confident that applications and devotion to duty will obviate a long training period.

As my resume shows, prior to my present position, this writer worked at XYZ Corporation as an assistant facilitator. In that position this writer learned to interface with personnel at different levels of the organizational ladder. Due to the fact of this experience, I learned in a labor intensive way that the bottom line is effectuated by skillful conceptualization.

Hoping to hear from you at an early date with reference to my application, this writer remains,

Your Humble Servant,

# SOFTWARE APPLICATION 6

Use this application, which provides template samples of *direct pattern* and *persuasive* cover letters, to create cover letters that you can edit and adapt for your own use.

CHAPTER

5

# Preparing for Your Interview

**OBJECTIVES**

**After you have studied this chapter, you should be able to:**

- Discover what you can learn about the company and the job from your interview.

- Focus on your strengths and project an air of confidence to help develop a positive attitude.

- Determine what the interviewer is really looking for.

- Dress appropriately for your interview.

Some people find the idea of a job interview frightening. This is especially true of young people who have relatively little experience in being interviewed and older people who are returning to the job market or who are changing careers and have not been on an interview for many years.

People in situations like these often wonder: What kind of questions will they ask me? Will everything go all right? Will I get the job? One of the things that will help you get the job is an aura of self-confidence. Yet, you cannot successfully project this image of self-confidence unless you actually feel it. Knowing what to expect on a job interview will help build your confidence. This chapter will tell you what to expect from an interview, and how to prepare for it.

## THE PURPOSE OF THE JOB INTERVIEW

You may think that the purpose of an interview is for the prospective employer to determine whether you have the skills required for the job. That is part of the purpose, but there is more to it.

The prospective employer wants to learn not just what kinds of skills you have but also what sort of a person you are. If you are applying for a position in management, for example, the employer wants to learn whether you have any management experience or training.

The employer also wants to learn about your management style. For example, are you authoritarian or democratic in dealing with subordinates? And will that management style, whatever it is, fit into the **corporate personality** (the distinct personality of a company)? You may be a good leader in one company, but your style of leadership might not fit as well into another organization.

To give another example, let's say that a company is going to interview you for a secretarial position. It wants an individual who can type accurately and answer the telephone pleasantly, of course. In some positions, however, the employer might also need a secretary who can work alone in the office. In such a situation, you will need to be a self-starter—a person who can take the responsibility and make decisions. An important purpose in such a job interview would be to determine whether you possess these personal characteristics along with the specific job skills.

Another purpose of the interview is for you to determine if the position meets your needs. As the company is checking you out, you are also checking out the company.

The interview provides an opportunity for you to find out what kind of tasks need to be performed on a day-to-day basis and to get a sense of the company's future. For example, are there likely to be opportunities for advancement?

If you are being interviewed by the person who would be your supervisor, you have an opportunity to decide whether you would feel comfortable working for this individual. Even if your interviewer is not going to be your supervisor, he or she still represents the company. This helps you to form an opinion as to what the company is like, so that you can ask yourself whether you want to work there. Although the company can reject you, you can also reject the company.

The purpose of a job interview is both to allow an employer to judge an applicant's character as well as to give an applicant the opportunity to decide whether a position or company is right for him or her.

# ACTIVITY 5-1

List six things other than salary or benefits that you would like to know about a company before you consider working for it.

_____

_____

_____

_____

_____

_____

# ACTIVITY 5-2

If you have worked part- or full-time, describe the corporate personality of a company you worked for. If you have never worked for any kind of business, describe the personality of a school you have attended.

_____

_____

_____

_____

_____

## DEVELOPING CONFIDENCE

When you go out on a job interview, there is bound to be at least a little bit of doubt. Even if you are confident of your ability to do the job, you can rarely be sure that you have precisely the qualifications a particular company is looking for.

However, one of the things employers look for in prospective employees is confidence. If you don't seem sure of yourself, then your prospective employer will probably not be too sure either.

How, then, do you muster up this aura of confidence, especially if somewhere inside you there is at least a little bit of self-doubt? Here are three things you can do that will help you to develop your confidence as you go out on a job interview.

### FOCUS ON YOUR STRENGTHS

Let's say you're not perfect in every way for the job in which you're interested. You know what? Neither is anyone else. We all have strengths and weaknesses that we bring to every job. If we don't have a lot of experience in an area we're applying for, we might have had some recent training in that area or related work experience. For example, even if you haven't dealt with the public in direct sales, you may have dealt with people as a receptionist.

Think about your strengths and about the qualities, skills, experiences, and training that you have to offer to the company that is interviewing you.

# ACTIVITY 5-3

Write down the title of a job you would like to have. Underneath it, list at least half a dozen strengths, qualities, skills, experiences, etc., that you would bring to that job. In making your list, be kind and generous to yourself.

Job Title _____

Strengths _____

_____

_____

_____

_____

_____

_____

Confidence is a key characteristic sought by employers in prospective employees. The job applicant who greets an employer with a positive attitude projects a self-assuredness that helps to convince the employer that this individual is both competent and in control.

## ACT CONFIDENT

Years ago, I took a Dale Carnegie sales course. Several times at every session the instructor had all the class members stand on their tip toes, point toward the ceiling, and shout, "*Look* enthusiastic and you'll *be* enthusiastic!" To tell you the truth, I always felt stupid when we had to do this. Nevertheless, I believe the underlying principle is true. The way we *act* influences the way we *feel*.

According to one school of psychology, when you laugh, the laughter itself makes you even happier. When you become angry and start yelling and shaking your fists, your own angry actions intensify the anger you feel. You can use this same principle to bolster your feelings of self-confidence. If you act in a self-confident manner, you will begin to feel more confident.

When you walk into the room where your interview is to be held, walk in confidently, with your shoulders back and your head up. Smile at the interviewer, speak right up when you are introduced, and shake hands firmly and confidently. All of these things will make you both *look* more confident and *feel* more confident.

During the interview itself, maintain good eye contact with the interviewer. Answer questions directly, assuredly, and honestly. These things will help you to come across as more confident.

If you act with confidence, you will feel more confident.

# ACTIVITY 5-4

Do some role playing, taking turns interviewing other class members in mock job interviews. In your interview, try to project a strong air of self-confidence.

## PUT YOUR INTERVIEW INTO PERSPECTIVE

One of the reasons that people sometimes become too tense when they are interviewed for a job is that they invest too much psychic energy in the interview. Suppose I don't get the job? they ask. What will I do then?

One way to help overcome the kind of nervous feeling that such doubts inevitably generate is to put the interview into perspective. If you don't get the job offer, it's not the end of the world. After all, if the company is interviewing just four candidates for a position, you have only a 25 percent chance of being offered the job. If 10 candidates are being interviewed, your chances drop to 10 percent. Most people have to go on several job interviews before they get a job offer. You can't get a job offer every time you go on an interview any more than a sales representative can make a sale each time she calls on a customer or a baseball player can hit a home run every time he steps up to bat.

We all come in second, third, or fourth best sometimes. If you expect that and prepare for it, you won't be crushed when you are not offered a job. You cannot afford to think that a failure to get a job offer is a rejection of you as a human being.

Your individual failure just means that someone else fit into the company a little better. You need to prepare for this, accept it when it happens, learn from it if you can, and then go on to your next interview.

# ACTIVITY 5-5

Suppose you go on an interview and are not offered the job. Write down what your next step would be.

_____

_____

_____

_____

_____

_____

## WHAT IS THE INTERVIEWER LOOKING FOR?

Before you are invited in for a job interview, the interviewer will normally have seen your resume and cover letter. He or she will already know quite a lot about you, so why do they have to bother with the interview?

To answer that question, let me recount a conversation I had with someone when we were working together on a team that was interviewing job candidates. My colleague referred to one candidate, saying, "He looks good on paper, but we had better talk to him to make sure he doesn't have two heads."

What did my colleague mean by those expressions? He meant that the man's resume was impressive, but we would still have to talk to him to find out what kind of a person he was. Did he have any kind of strange personality quirk or mannerism that we would be able to detect in the interview?

The position for which we were interviewing required someone who could relate to people well. We wanted to see if this candidate seemed to be the kind of person who would relate easily to people.

The interviewer knows a lot about your education and experience from your resume, cover letter, and the application form that you filled out before your interview. From the interview itself, the company hopes to confirm what it sees on paper. It also wants to know more about what kind of a person you are, how well your personality will fit the opening it has available, and how well your personality will fit the corporate personality.

Here are some of the specific traits that the interviewer might look for. As you read these, keep in mind that some traits are going to be more important than others, depending on the kind of position for which you are applying.

- *Analytical ability.* Can you gather information from various sources and put it together to see relationships and draw logical conclusions?

- *Assertiveness and confidence.* Are you willing to take initiative, take risks? Do you have confidence and a positive attitude?

- *Communications skills.* Do you listen well and respond clearly? Can you write clear records and reports?

- *Organizational ability.* Do you plan and organize your activities? Can you adapt to change without losing efficiency?

- *Interpersonal skills.* Can you work well with co-workers and the public? Are you sensitive to the feelings of others? Can you gain the confidence of other people?

- *Intellectual ability.* Can you process information and analyze problems with an open mind? Can you develop new ideas and grasp new situations?

- *Responsibility and maturity.* Do you do a thorough job and complete tasks on time? Can you work under pressure?

- *Decision-making ability.* Do you take a problem-solving approach to situations at work? Can you perceive and evaluate alternative methods? Can you make and implement appropriate decisions?

FRANK & ERNEST® by Bob Thaves

EMPLOYMENT COUNSELING

WE CALL IT A RESUME AND INTERVIEW, MISTER FREEBLE, NOT "SHOW AND TELL".

THAVES 3-7

FRANK & ERNEST reprinted by permission of NEA, Inc.

# ACTIVITY 5-6

List a title of a job in which you are interested. Next, list the personal attributes that would be required for the job. Opposite the attributes briefly describe what you have done to demonstrate that attitude.

EXAMPLE                                   Demonstration
Attribute                                 Wrote weekly reports at XYZ
Communication skill                       Corp.

JOB TITLE _____
Attribute                                 Demonstration

_____          _____

_____          _____

_____          _____

_____          _____

_____          _____

## FINAL PREPARATIONS FOR YOUR INTERVIEW

Before you go to an interview, learn something about the company. If you're not familiar with the company, ask someone who might know something about it or go to the library and look it up. *The Reader's Guide* and *Business Index* can direct you to magazines that focus on larger companies. Local business magazines and the business section of local newspapers will give you information about companies in your area. These sources can be very helpful as you look for information about companies that interest you.

Interviewers frequently ask questions such as: What do you know about our company? Why do you want to work for this company? If you have a ready answer for questions like these, you'll make a much better impression. It will show that you're truly interested in the company or that you're ambitious enough to do a little digging. You also will feel more confident if you go into the interview with some knowledge about the company to which you're applying.

When you want to make a good impression, dress up a bit and take a little extra care of your grooming. Make sure your fingernails are clean, your shoes are shined, and your clothes are pressed. But what kind of clothes should you wear to an interview?

You need to dress a little conservatively for the job interview. You should come to the interview dressed the way you would dress for the job you want. If you're not sure how people dress for work at a particular company, go there a day or two before the interview and observe its employees. If the dress at a particular company is fairly casual, however, remember that your interview is not just an ordinary work day. Dress up a little more than the people who already work there.

For most jobs in business, you will want to wear something conservative. That means a blue or gray suit for men, with a white shirt and conservative tie. Women have a wider choice of color, although they should avoid anything that is flashy. Women should wear skirts rather than slacks to the interview, and they should not wear too much makeup or jewelry. They should carry either a purse or a briefcase, but not both.

# ACTIVITY 5-7

Research at least two companies in your area. You can find information about the company by researching it in the library or by talking to one or more people who work for that company.

Try to find out things about the company's personality. What kind of workplace environment does the company have? Is there good communication between management and workers? What management style does the company practice? Rigid? Laid-back? Formal? Informal? Authoritarian? Democratic? Do people work together easily in the company or is there a lot of internal conflict?

Write a report about the company's corporate personality; then write why you think you might or might not fit into that company.

Write down 10 facts that you have discovered about the company. You might include information about the company's products or services, any new developments in the company, information about company personnel or history, or plans and predictions about the company's future.

_____
_____
_____
_____
_____
_____
_____
_____
_____
_____
_____

# ACTIVITY 5-8

List below the job title of a position for which you might go on an interview. Then describe the clothes you would wear to the interview. In your description, include colors, patterns, and accessories, including shoes, ties, purses, jewelry, etc.

Job Title _____
_____
_____
_____
_____
_____
_____
_____

# Making a Good Impression During Your Interview

**OBJECTIVES**

After you have studied this chapter, you should be able to

- Prepare a work history sheet to help you fill out an employment application.

- Make out a reference sheet.

- Prepare yourself for different kinds of interviews and interviewers.

- Give appropriate answers to the kinds of questions that are frequently asked in an interview.

- Respond effectively if an illegal question is asked.

In this chapter you will learn how to prepare for your interview as well as how to make a good initial impression. You will also learn about the different types of interviewers and interviews. Some interviewers are easy to talk to, whereas others are considerably more difficult. By understanding what motivates each type of interviewer, you will be able to relate to them more effectively. You will learn what you need to bring with you to your interview as well so that you can fill out an application form completely and accurately.

This chapter also contains a list of 36 questions asked in interviews. Knowing ahead of time what questions might be asked will help you to prepare more effective answers. In addition, this chapter looks at questions that may not legally be asked and tells you how to respond if you are asked such questions.

## ARRIVING FOR YOUR INTERVIEW

First impressions are long-lasting. If you arrive ten minutes, or even five minutes, late for your interview, you will not make a good first impression.

Be sure that you know how to get to the place where your interview is. If you're unsure, make the trip a day or so ahead of time so you'll know where you're going and how long it takes to get there. When setting out for the interview itself, give yourself some extra time to allow for traffic delays and the other little pitfalls that are part of everyday life. It is always a good idea to arrive a few minutes early because in many interview situations, you will be asked to fill out a job **application form**, providing information about your work history and education, before your interview begins.

Because you might be asked to fill out a job application form, you should be able to provide any work history information that might be asked for. Do you remember the dates of your past jobs? Your work supervisors' names? Do you remember the telephone number of the company you worked for eight years ago? If you think you might not remember any of this information, it is a good

## EMPLOYMENT HISTORY

| Employer Name/Address/Telephone | Dates First Last | Supervisor | Job Title | Major Duties |
|---|---|---|---|---|
| | | | | |
| | | | | |
| | | | | |
| | | | | |

**Figure 6–1.** A Work History Sheet

idea to prepare a **work history sheet** on a slip of paper or a card that you can carry in your purse or wallet. (See Figure 6-1.)

You will also need to bring a **reference sheet** with you. This is a piece of paper that contains the names, job titles, work addresses, and day-time telephone numbers of the people whom you are listing as references. (See Figure 6-2.) You may need this information for your application form or if your interviewer asks you for references. If you have a reference sheet prepared ahead of time, you can just hand it to your interviewer.

An employer is interested only in work references. The best references are people who know something about your work and can give an unbiased account of your work habits. This includes both present and previous supervisors and employers. If you have been in school recently, you can also use present and previous teachers as references. Of course, you must ask permission ahead of time if you intend to use someone as a reference.

When you fill out your application form, do so neatly and completely. (See Figure 6-3.) Don't leave any blank spaces. If there is a section of the application

---

**Reference Sheet for
Marie Belanger
421 Auburn St.
Portland, ME 04103
555-1212**

Mr. Peter Loring
Service Manager
Kemco, Inc.
1024 Forest Ave.
Portland, ME 04103
555-7473

Dr. Susan Ruggiero
Business Professor
Casco Bay College
477 Congress St.
Portland, ME 04101
555-0196

Ms. Deborah Pelletier
Office Manager
Green Insurance Company
827 Broadway
South Portland, ME 04106
555-2137

Mr. David Turgeon
English Teacher
Gorham High School
41 Morrill Avenue
Gorham, ME 04036
555-5052

**Figure 6–2.** A Reference Sheet

## AMERICAN PHARMACIES EMPLOYMENT APPLICATION I

### AN EQUAL OPPORTUNITY EMPLOYER

**PERSONAL INFORMATION**                DATE _____ / _____ / _____

NAME _____ SOCIAL SECURITY NO. _____
     (Last)          (First)         (M.I.)

ADDRESS _____
      (Street)         (City)        (State)        (Zip)

TELEPHONE ( _____ ) _____

ARE YOU:

☐ YES ☐ NO    OVER THE AGE OF 18? IF NO, PLEASE STATE YOUR AGE _____

☐ YES ☐ NO    A PREVIOUS APPLICANT? IF YES, WHEN _____ / _____ / _____ WHERE _____

☐ YES ☐ NO    A PREVIOUS EMPLOYEE OF AMERICAN PHARMACIES?

           YES,

           FROM _____ TO _____ LOCATION _____ DIVISION _____

☐ YES ☐ NO    ELIGIBLE TO WORK IN THE UNITED STATES? (Proof of citizenship or immigration status will be required upon employment.)

POSITION APPLIED FOR _____ PART-TIME ☐   FULL-TIME ☐

WAGES REQUIRED _____ /HOUR

SPECIFY ALL DAYS AND HOURS AVAILABLE    ☐ ANY-DAY ANY-HOUR

SUNDAY _____ MONDAY _____ TUESDAY _____ WEDNESDAY _____

THURSDAY _____ FRIDAY _____ SATURDAY _____ HOLIDAYS _____

HOW REFERRED? ☐ SELF ☐ EMPLOYEE ☐ STORE SIGN ☐ NEWSPAPER ☐ OTHER (specify) _____

PLEASE LIST 2 PERSONAL AND/OR CHARACTER REFERENCES (not including relatives)

NAME _____ TELEPHONE # _____

ADDRESS _____
      (Street)         (City)        (State)        (Zip)

HOW DO YOU KNOW THIS PERSON? _____

NAME _____ TELEPHONE # _____

ADDRESS _____
      (Street)         (City)        (State)        (Zip)

HOW DO YOU KNOW THIS PERSON? _____

### EMPLOYMENT RELATED INFORMATION

Please list any relatives currently employed at **American Pharmacies**. (Include name, store, department)

Do you have any physical, mental, or medical impairments which would interfere with your ability to perform job-related functions?*

Have you been convicted of a job-related crime within the last 5 years? If yes, please explain: (A conviction may be relevant if job-related but may not bar you from employment.)

### EDUCATION AND RELATED TRAINING

CIRCLE LAST YEAR OF SCHOOL COMPLETED: HIGH SCHOOL: 9 10 11 12    COLLEGE: FR. SO. JR. SR.

PLEASE LIST ANY OTHER EDUCATION, TRAINING, CERTIFICATES OR SPECIAL SKILLS THAT YOU POSSESS THAT ARE RELATED TO THE JOB FOR WHICH YOU ARE APPLYING: _____

OPR-46 Item #450056 Revised 2-12-91                                 P/#731313

**Figure 6–3.** An Employment Application

## EMPLOYMENT AND EXPERIENCE

BEGINNING WITH YOUR PRESENT OR MOST RECENT EXPERIENCE, LIST YOUR LAST 3 EMPLOYERS, ASSIGMENTS OR VOLUNTEER ACTIVITIES INCLUDING MILITARY EXPERIENCE.

| PRESENT/LAST EMPLOYER | | TYPE OF BUSINESS | ADDRESS | PHONE NUMBER ( ) |
| --- | --- | --- | --- | --- |
| START DATE | LEAVE DATE | SALARY | REASON FOR LEAVING | |
| JOB TITLE | | SUPERVISOR AND TITLE | | MAY WE CONTACT? ☐ Yes ☐ No |
| DESCRIPTION OF JOB AND RESPONSIBILITIES | | | | |

| PREVIOUS EMPLOYER | | TYPE OF BUSINESS | ADDRESS | PHONE NUMBER ( ) |
| --- | --- | --- | --- | --- |
| START DATE | LEAVE DATE | SALARY | REASON FOR LEAVING | |
| JOB TITLE | | SUPERVISOR AND TITLE | | MAY WE CONTACT? ☐ Yes ☐ No |
| DESCRIPTION OF JOB AND RESPONSIBILITIES | | | | |

| PREVIOUS EMPLOYER | | TYPE OF BUSINESS | ADDRESS | PHONE NUMBER ( ) |
| --- | --- | --- | --- | --- |
| START DATE | LEAVE DATE | SALARY | REASON FOR LEAVING | |
| JOB TITLE | | SUPERVISOR AND TITLE | | MAY WE CONTACT? ☐ Yes ☐ No |
| DESCRIPTION OF JOB AND RESPONSIBILITIES | | | | |

COMMENTS: (Including explanation of any gaps in employment and any reasons you have for wishing us not to contact any employers listed above.)

OTHER QUALIFICATIONS: If there is any other information you would like to add which may help us to evaluate your qualifications for the job for which you are applying, please explain:

**PLEASE READ CAREFULLY BEFORE SIGNING BELOW.**

I Certify that answers given herin are true and complete to the best of my knowledge. I authorize an investigation of all statements contained in this application for employment and hereby consent to your obtaining reports from previous employers, schools, and personal references. Only job related information will be requested or considered in evaluating my employment application.

In the event I am employed, I understand that the terms and conditions of my employment may be improved, or otherwise changed, from time to time by **American Pharmacies** without prior notice and that no individual contract of employment can be established at any time between any employee of **American Pharmacies** and the Company other than by an express written agreement signed by an officer of **American Pharmacies**. Furthermore, I understand that any falsification, misrepresentation, or deliberate omission of information made by me on this application will be cause for immediate dismissal.

I understand that this application will remain effective for 90 days and must be renewed in writing, in person, in order for me to be considered for employment.

Signature of Applicant _____ Date _____

THANK YOU FOR YOUR APPLICATION

| FOR OFFICE USE ONLY | |
| --- | --- |
| ☐ A COMMENTS: _____ | DATE: _____ |
| ☐ I _____ | INTERVIEWER _____ |

**Figure 6–3.** Continued

form that clearly doesn't apply to you, write N/A (not applicable). Some companies throw out any application form that has not been filled out completely.

It is equally important to write neatly on your application form. This is a sample of the kind of work you do. A neat, legible application form creates a good impression.

# ACTIVITY 6-1

Make out a work history sheet containing any information that you might need to put on an application form. This would include dates of past employment, job titles and duties, names of work supervisors, and addresses and telephone numbers of companies you worked for.

# ACTIVITY 6-2

Make out a reference sheet. Get permission from three or four people to use their names as references. They should be people who know something about your work and who would give you a good reference. It is more persuasive to use people whose job titles sound authoritative. Type up the reference sheet with names, job titles, work addresses, and telephone numbers of the people whose names you are using. Make photocopies of the reference sheet so you can take one to each job interview.

## TYPES OF INTERVIEWERS AND INTERVIEWS

In my work at Casco Bay College's Job Placement Seminar, I've had the opportunity to observe many interviews over the years. One of the things I've noticed is that there are as many different interview styles as there are interviewers. Most interviewers fall into certain patterns. Here are some:

### RELAXING OR HOT SEAT START

Competent, experienced interviewers know that most job applicants are at least a little nervous. These interviewers try to help applicants overcome their nervousness by asking a casual question, making a casual comment, or even by telling a little joke. This is called an "ice breaker," and it helps the applicant to relax a bit and feel that the interviewer is not going to be some kind of ogre.

I have seen interviewers (only a few) who do things such as deliberately arrive five or ten minutes late for the interview themselves. Then they'll take another two or three minutes (although it seems like longer) to look over an applicant's resume before beginning the interview. What do you do while the interviewer is looking over your resume? Twiddle your thumbs? Play with the buttons on your jacket? Sitting there without being asked a question is likely to make a person who is already uneasy feel even less sure, more nervous, and more uncomfortable.

It might help if you know why your interviewer is beginning the interview this way. There are two possible explanations. One is that you are being given what is called a **stress interview**. The interviewer may be deliberately putting you under stress to see how you will respond. This is a legitimate tactic only if the job for which you are applying is one that carries a lot of stress. If the job is not very stressful and the interviewer is nonetheless conducting a stress interview, you might ask yourself whether you want to work for that person. Remember, part of the purpose of the interview is for *you* to check out the company.

THE FAR SIDE          By GARY LARSON

Let's see...You make fire--good... You make tools--good...You hunt mammoth...oKaaaaaay.. Uh-oh! Your references are all baboons..not good.

Primitive resumes

Reprinted with permission of Universal Press Syndicate.

A more likely explanation for an interview that begins this way is that the interviewer is not very skilled. In either case, if you are interested in the job, relax as much as you're able and don't let your interviewer throw you.

## EASY, TOUGH, OR NASTY

Some interviewers are so warm and friendly that your interview may seem like a pleasant social encounter. They make you feel that you have done them a favor by coming in and telling them about your qualifications for the position.

Other interviewers, although they may be pleasant enough, will put you on the spot a number of times during the interview. They'll do this by asking questions that are really tough to answer: What is your major weakness? Why should I hire you? What can you offer this company? Did you ever have a boss you couldn't get along with? (The answer to this last question, incidentally, should always be "No.")

If you understand why the interviewer asks such questions, and you have enough confidence in yourself, you'll be able to respond more easily. It also helps if you are prepared ahead of time for these tough questions. In the next section of this chapter you will find a list of questions frequently asked in job interviews.

Most of the interviewers I have observed tended to be tough rather than easy. They may have been friendly and warm, and they may have helped the applicant to relax a bit, but sometime before the interview was over they asked a question that put the applicant on the spot unless some thought had been given ahead of time as to how the question could be answered.

## SKILLED OR UNSKILLED

People with experience in interviewing have developed techniques to learn what they need to know about applicants to make informed hiring decisions. Sometimes, however, an interview may be conducted by someone who is relatively inexperienced and unskilled in interview techniques. The owner and manager of a small company, for example, may not have extensive experience in interviewing. In other instances, a committee of people who work for an organization may conduct an interview. Typically, the committee members will know something about the job but not much about conducting an interview.

If your interviewer seems unskilled or unsure of himself or herself, *you* can take a more active role in the interview. Don't let your interviewer's inexperience throw you off. Recognize that he or she may also feel a bit nervous and that you can help your interviewer feel more comfortable by smiling, being friendly, and acting at ease. If your interviewer doesn't ask you about some important qualifications that you have, volunteer that information.

## INDIVIDUAL OR GROUP

Most interviews are conducted by one person, but I have seen several that were conducted by a group. Some people are intimidated by the thought of having a group of people ask them questions. However, the same principles apply whether the interview is being conducted by one person or six.

There are, however, two major differences between an individual and a **group interview**. The first is that the group is almost sure to be made up primarily of people who are inexperienced in interviewing. For example, I've seen a number of group interviews in education and other fields. Most of the interviewers were teachers who were on a faculty search committee. In such situations, there is always at least one person who is experienced in interviewing—such as a dean, a department head, or a superintendent. This person is usually in charge of the interview. I have seen interviews of this type where the members of the group had a list of questions and took turns asking them. This list of questions helped to keep the interview more structured.

The role of the group members, aside from the group leader, is primarily to evaluate and react. Sometime after the interview, the group gets together and shares their impressions of the candidates they have interviewed.

This leads to the second major difference between the individual and the group interview. When you are being interviewed by one person, you must make a good impression on that person. When a group is involved, however, you have to make a favorable impression on all members of the group. This is further complicated by the fact that different individuals in the group will have different interests, values, and ways of looking at things.

When you are being interviewed by a group, you must be particularly alert to body language signals given off by the various members of the group. You should be able to sense whether a particular answer you have given was adequate in response to the real question in the interviewer's mind. For example, if the interviewer asks you how you got along with your previous boss, the real question might be: Can you take supervision and follow directions? And if you sense the answer was not adequate, then you need to elaborate.

# ACTIVITY 6-3

Do some role playing. Take turns interviewing other class members. When you play the role of interviewer, ask several tough questions.

# ACTIVITY 6-4

Form a group that will interview several students playing the role of job applicants. Decide ahead of time what questions each group member will ask. Also decide what, specifically, each group member will be looking for in the candidate. Make these decisions while the candidate is out of the room.

## QUESTIONS FREQUENTLY ASKED IN AN INTERVIEW

In Figure 6-4 you will find a list of questions that interviewers frequently ask. If you are familiar with these questions, you'll be less likely to be taken by surprise when the interviewer asks a probing question.

As you look at these questions, try to figure out the purpose behind each one. Numbers 3, 14, 27, and 33, for example, are intended to learn about your future plans. Numbers 2, 4, 5, 9, and 16 are designed to find out how much you know about the company and the general field of work. A number of other questions seek to discover your view of yourself. For example, the interviewer might want to learn how confident and mature you are or whether you feel you can work independently or require a lot of supervision.

Read through this list and analyze each question. There is no right answer to any question. Think about how you would answer each question if it were asked of you. The best answer is usually the most honest answer, but use common sense. I heard one interviewer ask a job applicant what he planned to be doing in five years. The applicant told him that he planned to be working in another field. That answer did not show common sense nor did it get the applicant the job.

I know of another applicant who was asked why she wanted to change jobs. She told her interviewer that the work pace at her old job had picked up and she no longer had time to read on the job. Needless to say, her interviewer didn't give her an opportunity to read on the new job either.

Here is one more situation where you need to be prudent when you respond to a question. Often the reason you may want to change jobs is that you are having problems with your boss. If you are asked why you want to change jobs, *never* say it is because you don't get along with your boss, even though that may be true and even if you've never had any problems with any other boss you've ever worked for.

Interviewers, after all, have a very short time in which to make a judgment as to how well you will work out on the job. If you say you don't get along with your boss, it will raise a red flag in the interviewer's mind. Your interviewer has no way of knowing who is the source of the problem between you and your boss. From his or her point of view, the source of difficulty could just as easily be you as it could be your boss.

Be aware that these questions and answers often lead to follow-up questions. If you are asked to name your major strength, for example, you may very well be asked to provide an example of a way in which that strength has been an asset at work. If you are asked to name your biggest weakness, expect a follow-up question asking what you have done to overcome that weakness.

# ACTIVITY 6-5

Look carefully at the questions in Figure 6-4. Decide what you would say in response to all of them. Think about a possible follow-up to each question and decide how you would reply.

## WHAT YOUR INTERVIEWER MAY AND MAY NOT ASK

Your interviewer may not ask an applicant **illegal questions** about ethnic background, religion, or marital status. Unless the questions are clearly job related, your interviewer also may not ask about age or physical condition. Your interviewer may not ask, for example, whether you have any physical handicaps. It is permissible, however, to ask if you have any physical problems that would interfere with your performance of the job.

Your interviewer may not ask whether you're married, have children, or plan to have children. It is not legal to ask what religious holidays you observe or to ask personal data such as your weight and height, unless they are clearly related to the job for which you are applying.

An employer may ask about your educational background, employment history, and specific job skills, but may not ask whether you have ever been fired from a job, unless it can be proved that the question is job-related.

What should you do if your interviewer asks you an illegal question? First of all, you must recognize that if an interviewer asks such a question, it is probably out of ignorance. Anyone experienced in human resources knows what kind of questions are illegal.

With this point clarified, here are some things *not* to do if an employer asks you an illegal question:

1. Don't remain silent or reply that you prefer not to answer the question. If your interviewer doesn't know that an illegal question has been asked, he or she will be puzzled by your silence or refusal to respond.

2. Don't tell your interviewer that the question is illegal and may not be asked. Remember, the question has probably been asked out of ignorance. If you suddenly accuse your interviewer of an illegal act, he or she will probably find a "good" reason not to offer the job to you.

1. In what type of position are you most interested?

2. Why do you think you might like to work for this company?

3. What are your future vocational plans?

4. Why did you choose your particular field of work?

5. What do you know about our company?

6. What qualifications do you have that make you feel you will be successful in your field?

7. What do you think determines a person's progress in a company?

8. What personal characteristics are necessary for success in your chosen field?

9. Why do you think you would like this particular kind of work?

10. What interests you about our product or service?

11. What is your major weakness? Your major strength?

12. Are you willing to go where the company sends you?

13. Do you prefer any particular geographic location?

14. What job in our company do you want to work toward?

15. Would you prefer to work in a large or small company?

16. What is your impressionof how this industry operates today?

17. What are the disadvantages of your chosen field?

18. What have you done that shows initiative and a willingness to work?

19. In what school activities have you participated? Which did you enjoy most?

20. What jobs have you held? How were they obtained and why did you leave?

21. What courses did you like best in school? Least? Why?

22. What percentage of your college expenses did you earn? How?

23. Do you feel that you have received a good general training?

24. What extracurricular offices have you held?

25. What are your salary requirements?

26. If you were starting college again, what courses would you take?

27. How much money do you hope to earn at age 30? 35?

28. Why did you decide to go to the school that you went to?

29. How did you rank in your graduating class in high school? College?

30. Do you prefer to work with others or by yourself?

31. Do you like routine work?

32. Do you like regular hours?

33. Do you have plans for continuing your education?

34. What kind of people "rub you the wrong way"?

35. What are your own special abilities?

36. Do you like to travel?

**Figure 6–4.** Frequently Asked Interview Questions

Of course, you can go ahead and answer the question. If you believe the question was asked innocently and that a direct answer won't hurt you, you can just go ahead and answer it. There are, however, tactful ways to respond to such questions without giving a direct answer.

## EFFECTIVE ANSWERS TO ILLEGAL QUESTIONS

One way to respond to an illegal question is to say something such as, "I'm not sure how that relates to my ability to handle the job. Could you clarify it for me?"

An even better answer is to respond to the fear behind the question. For example, if the interviewer asks you whether you have any children, the fear might be that you will miss work if your children are sick. You can respond to this fear by making specific reference to your regular attendance at a present or previous job.

# ACTIVITY 6-6

1. An interviewer asks a young woman if she has any children. The young woman knows that the question is illegal. Should she simply say that it is not legal to ask that question? Why or why not?

   _____

   _____

   _____

   _____

2. Write a more effective response for the young woman to make to an illegal question about children.

   _____

   _____

   _____

   _____

## IF YOU DON'T GET THE JOB

If you don't get the job, don't take it as a personal rejection. Perhaps you didn't fit the pattern the employer was looking for. Perhaps you wouldn't have liked the job if they had hired you.

If you feel you had the necessary qualifications and you did well in the interview but still didn't get the job, it is all right to call the individual who conducted the interview and ask if he or she can give you some suggestions for the next time you go out on an interview. Ask it in this way. Don't say, "What did I do wrong?" That kind of question puts the interviewer on the defensive. Chances are, however, that you didn't do anything wrong. Someone else probably had more experience, an extra qualification, or in some way fit better into the opening.

Recognize that few people get the first job for which they interview. Most people have to go on several interviews before they come to the job that is right for them. When they come away from that interview, chances are they will get a job offer.

# ACTIVITY 6-7

Talk to someone who has been turned down for a job, or use your own experience if you have been turned down yourself. Why does the person who was turned down think that he or she did not get the job?

Try to find someone who has done some hiring. Ask that person for some of the reasons that job applicants were not hired. If you work part-time, your own boss might be able to supply that information for you. Your teacher might be able to suggest other leads.

When you have gathered some information about reasons for being turned down for a job, share it with the rest of the class.

# CHAPTER

# Writing a Good Follow-Up Letter

## OBJECTIVES

After you have studied this chapter, you should be able to

- Write an effective thank-you letter after a job interview.

- Write a follow-up letter some months after being turned down for a job to inquire whether the situation at the employer's company has changed in the interim.

- Write a thank-you letter after being turned down for a job to keep the door open for possible future employment.

There are several types of follow-up letters that you might write after an interview. These are primarily direct pattern letters and are easy to write. An effective follow-up letter can sometimes make the difference between getting the job and not getting it.

## THE THANK-YOU LETTER

The most important letter to write after your interview is a **thank-you letter,** thanking the prospective employer for the interview. This letter is an expected courtesy. It is also a chance to reaffirm your interest in the job and possibly to add something about your qualifications that you might have omitted in your interview.

It is important to write the thank-you letter right away. If your interviewer has talked to a number of candidates, a thank-you letter from you will help you to stand out in the interviewer's mind. If your interviewer is trying to decide whether to offer the job to you or to someone else, a thank-you letter might be all that is needed to sway the decision in your favor.

The thank-you letter shown in Figure 7-1, written by Harry Dexter to Holly Columbine, makes reference to things that have been discussed in the interview as well as things that Harry has learned during the interview. It affirms his interest in working for the company and implies that he is ambitious and hard-working.

## ACTIVITY 7-1

Name two ways in which a thank-you letter might help you get a job.

_____

_____

_____

_____

```
RFD #1, Box 214
Saco, ME  04072

May 23, 199_


Ms. Holly Columbine
Marchand Travel Service
29 Coin St.
Portland, ME  04101

Dear Ms. Columbine:

Thank you very much for talking with me Wednesday about the travel consultant position
at Marchand Travel Service. What you had to say about the expanding market of the
travel industry made it clear to me that there is great opportunity for a travel consultant
who is ambitious and hard-working. I was certainly impressed with the professionalism
and the positive attitudes of the people whom I met at Marchand. I would very much like
to become a part of that team.

I will be looking forward to hearing from you after you have made a decision about my
application.

Cordially,

Harry Dexter

Harry Dexter
```

**Figure 7–1.** Harry Dexter's Thank-You Letter

Name two things that should be included in a thank-you letter.

_____
_____
_____
_____

# ACTIVITY 7-2

You have been interviewed by Mr. Ted Frankel for a job that interests you at Sotheby Enterprises. Think about something that you might have learned about Sotheby Enterprises during the interview. Then, write a letter to Mr. Frankel thanking him for the interview. Mention something favorable that you learned about the company during the interview. Let him know that you are interested in the position and imply, without sounding boastful, that you possess two or three of the major qualifications for which the company is looking.

## THE FOLLOW-UP LETTER

When people do not get a response to their applications, they will sometimes send a **follow-up letter.** A follow-up letter is one that is sent after the interview to affirm your interest in the job and to emphasize one or more of your qualifications. Follow-up letters may even be sent after you have been turned down for a job. In such a case, the follow-up letter can either keep a door open to you for possible future employment or it can be used to determine if the employment situation at the employer's company has changed. My advice to you is: Don't waste your time. If you haven't heard from a company after three or four weeks, it usually means that they have no opening for which you are qualified or they simply are not interested in your application. It is unlikely that a follow-up letter will create interest if the original resume and application did not.

However, there is another situation where a follow-up letter may be appropriate. I am referring to a letter after six months or a year. The situation at the company where you sent your application may very well have changed during that time. If you are still interested in working for the company, you might send them a follow-up letter that refers to your original application and let them know that you are still interested in working for them. The letter should include an update of your career since you first applied, particularly if there is something that has made you more qualified. For example, college courses, the completion of a college degree or course of training, or experience in your field would all make you a stronger candidate. The company may still have your resume, but it is a good idea to send them another copy, just in case they don't.

Kamal Hamdoun wrote such a follow-up letter to Beverly Samuels, the Director of Management Training of the Bank of Syracuse. Six months earlier, he had spoken to Tom Callahan, manager of the White Plains branch of the bank, about job possibilities, but this was an informational interview. He had then applied for their management training program, but was not accepted. Kamal has learned that a new management training group is about to begin, so he sends a follow-up letter (in this case, really a new application). He includes an updated resume because he has a new address, has been working on a new job for the past six months, and has taken a course in banking and finance. In his letter, shown in Figure 7-2, he refers to his new qualifications.

## ACTIVITY 7-3

What would be the point of writing a follow-up letter several months after you have been turned down for a position?

_____

_____

_____

_____

_____

_____

## ACTIVITY 7-4

Unfortunately, you didn't get the job at Sotheby Enterprises, but you felt that you were a strong candidate. In fact, when Mr. Frankel called to tell you that the job had been offered to someone else, he also told you that if there had been two openings, he would have offered one of them to you.

Write a letter to Mr. Frankel thanking him for considering you. Let him know that you are still interested in working for Sotheby Enterprises and that you would like to be considered if another opening occurs.

---

217 Amherst St.
Livonia, NY 14487

June 23, 199_

Ms. Tamara Samuels
Bank of Syracuse
1433 Ware Street
Syracuse, NY 13220

Dear Ms. Samuels:

After I talked last January with Mr. Tom Callahan, manager of the White Plains branch of the Bank of Syracuse, I decided that banking was the career for me. I was especially interested in working for the Bank of Syracuse. The bank's motto, "The Bank With a Human Face," impressed me.

As you may recall, I applied for the management training program but was not accepted. I took that not as a rejection or setback, but as an opportunity to better prepare myself for a position in the bank's management training program. To do this, I enrolled immediately in a course in banking and finance at the University of Rochester and took a position of department manager at the K-Mart in Rochester. I found the banking and finance course fascinating and have registered for a second banking course for this summer.

I feel that I am in a stronger position to offer something more to the Bank of Syracuse as a management trainee. With my six-months' experience in management, my course in banking, and my liberal arts background, I believe I can make a contribution to "The Bank With a Human Face." Please consider my reapplication for a position in the bank's management training program.

Sincerely,

*Kamal Hamdoun*

Kamal Hamdoun

**Figure 7–2.** Kamal Hamdoun's Follow-Up Letter

## THE I-DIDN'T-GET-THE-JOB-BUT-THANKS-ANYWAY LETTER

Usually you wouldn't write a letter in this type of situation. You applied for a job. They interviewed you, but decided to offer the job to someone else. End of story.

But wait! Maybe it isn't the end of the story. If the company hired someone else, they hired the person who in their best judgment was the most qualified for the position. However, sometimes things change. Maybe the person who was given the job decided after a month or so that she didn't like it. Or maybe the company was disappointed in his work. Possibly a similar opening occurs a few months later, and you may still be a good candidate for this position.

If you did not get the job you interviewed for, but you feel you were a strong candidate, the interview went well, and you are still interested in working for that company, you might write a follow-up letter.

Hannah Petersen wrote the letter shown in Figure 7-3 to Chris Craig, editor of the *Defiance Crescent News*, after the position she had applied for was offered to someone else.

Still another situation that might call for a follow-up letter after being turned down for a job would be one where you have been rejected because you didn't really have the qualifications, but the interviewer told you what you needed to

---

1467 Grove St.
Warren, MI  48091

May 14, 199_

Mr. Chris Craig
Editor
Defiance Crescent-News
Defiance, OH 43512

Dear Mr. Craig:

Of course I was disappointed to learn that you have offered the job of assistant editor of the *Defiance Crescent News* to someone else. I was pleased, however, that you had considered me for that position, despite my limited experience. I want you to know that I was impressed with what I saw at the *Crescent News*. I was impressed with the quality of writing in the paper. I liked the casual atmosphere in the editorial office. Despite this casual environment, everything seemed to get done smoothly and efficiently.

The *Defiance Crescent News* is definitely the kind of paper that I would like to work for. I hope you will keep my resume on file and consider me if another opening occurs in editing or reporting.

Sincerely,

Hannah Petersen

Hannah Petersen

**Figure 7-3.** Hannah Petersen's I-Didn't-Get-the-Job-But-Thank-You-Anyway Letter

143 Elm Street
Webster Groves, MO 63119

December 3, 199_

Ms. Maria Santiago
Director
St. Louis Cerebral Palsy Center
1287 Kingshighway
St. Louis, MO 63118

Dear Ms. Santiago:

I want to thank you for taking the time to interview me and tell me about some of the good work that is being done at the St. Louis Cerebral Palsy Center.

After talking with you, I understand why it is necessary to have more than simply a desire to become a social worker. I am going to follow your advice and take two more courses in social welfare during the second semester and then two more during the summer session. After that, I will apply for a provisional social worker's license.

Many thanks for your helpful suggestions.

Sincerely,

*Bruce Chang*

Bruce Chang

**Figure 7–4.** Bruce Chang's I-Didn't-Get-the-Job-But-Thank-You-Anyway Letter

do to meet them for future consideration. The letter by Bruce Chang to Maria Santiago, shown in Figure 7-4, is an example of this type of letter.

One final bit of advice. When you write any type of follow-up letter, be yourself and write in a conversational style. A conversational writing style will help you to reinforce the favorable image you presented in your interview.

# ACTIVITY 7-5

What would be the purpose of writing a thank-you letter if you didn't get the job?

_____

_____

_____

_____

# ACTIVITY 7-6

It has now been approximately six months since you had your interview with Mr. Frankel. Business has recently picked up for Sotheby Enterprises, and you think there might be an opening that you could fill. During these six months you have gained additional experience in your field by working in a part-time job.

Write a letter to Mr. Frankel. Tell him that you have further experience since the interview and you are still interested in working for Sotheby Enterprises. Mention in your letter that you are enclosing an updated resume.

# SOFTWARE APPLICATION 7

Use this application, which presents several types and purposes of follow-up letters, to practice writing each type, with samples provided for you to edit and adapt for your own purposes.

# Appendix A
# Model Resumes

On the following pages are 14 model resumes representing applicants in various fields of work. Additional model resumes can be found in other parts of this book. In Chapter 3, one or more resumes are provided for each of five job applicants. On pages 37 and 39, and again on pages 41 and 42, you will find two resumes for the same person, each resume geared toward a different career.

Although every occupation is not represented on the following pages, the resumes represent a broad spectrum of fields. Most of the areas of business are represented: secretarial, management, accounting, and sales. There are also resumes for education, social work, health care occupations, skilled trades, and technical fields.

The different careers, however, are less important than the specific situations of the applicants. The qualifications for a job as a Certified Nurse's Aide may be very different from those of an accountant, but the way those qualifications are listed on the resume may be the same for applicants in either career.

In considering what to include on your resume, you might find the life situation of the applicant to be much more important than the specific career. Several of the resumes are for current or recent college graduates. One of the resumes is for a man who wants to advance in his career (Hamilton Broadhurst). Another of the applicants at one time had his own business (Reuben Zamora).

As you look through these resumes, don't be too concerned with trying to find a resume that matches your career field. You'll find it more helpful, perhaps, to find resumes that match your career situation, whether you're just entering a career, getting ready to move up, or thinking about changing careers.

**COMPUTER PROGRAMMER**

**FRANK HARZOG**
2841 Columbine Avenue #11
Denver Colorado 80208
(303) 555-2891


**OBJECTIVE**

Seeking a position as an entry-level computer programmer

**EDUCATION**

Candidate for BA, University of Denver,
Denver CO, 199_
Major: Mathematics, Minor: Computer Programming

**Courses in Computer Programming and Mathematics**

| | |
|---|---|
| COBOL | Probability Theory |
| FORTRAN | Mathematical Analysis |
| BASIC | Statistics |
| RPG II | Finite Mathematics |
| Systems Management | Algorithmic |
| | Interface |
| Advanced Operating Systems | Calculus |
| | Trigonometry |

**PART-TIME AND SUMMER EXPERIENCE**

Computer Lab Supervisor, University of Denver
199_–199_ Academic year.
    Supervised work of beginning computer students

Data Entry Clerk, Denver National Bank, Denver CO
Summers of 199_ & 199_

**EXTRA-CURRICULAR ACTIVITIES**

Key Club
Barbershop quartet

**REFERENCES**

Available upon request

CONSTRUCTION FOREMAN

**REUBEN ZAMORA**
4241 Wentworth Boulevard
Indianapolis IN 46201
(317) 555-2424

## OBJECTIVE

Position as Construction Foreman

## EXPERIENCE

Construction Foreman, Hammond Construction Company, Hammond, IN
(1989—present)

* Supervised construction of homes in the Maude Simpkins
  and West Tyrone Developments
* Hired carpenters and checked their work
* Directed interior and exterior carpentry

Self-Employed Contractor, Hammond IN (1983—89)

* Built standard homes and small commercial buildings
* Worked with developers and subcontractors
* Hired and supervised carpenters and masons
* Purchased building materials and supplies
* Estimated jobs

Journeyman and Master Carpenter, Fort Wayne Building Company, Fort
Wayne, IN (1975—83)

* Assisted Master Carpenters
* Later was put in charge of journeyman carpenters building
  and remodeling homes
* Directed layout carpentry and flooring

## EDUCATION

Northern Indiana Technical Institute, South Bend, IN
Diploma in Building Trades, 1975

## REFERENCES

Available upon request

# CUSTOMER SERVICE REPRESENTATIVE

DIANE KWONG
758 Armstrong St. #3
Virginia Beach, VA 23452
(804) 555-3245

**OBJECTIVE** — Seeking a challenging position as a Customer Service Representative in a company that offers an opportunity for growth

## EMPLOYMENT EXPERIENCE

199_–present — Xanadu Manufacturing Company
Customer Service Representative
* Respond to customer correspondence
* Take care of customer problems over the telephone
* Enter orders into computer system and route them through the plant
* Maintain contact with sales representatives in the mid-Atlantic area

1989–199_ — Harbor Automotive Company
Customer Service Representative
* Employed as sales trainee, moved into Customer Service Department
* In charge of repair or replacement of defective parts

## EDUCATION

Virginia Technological Institute
15 credit hours in Business Administration

## REFERENCES

Available upon request

**DIETICIAN**

Marie St. Pierre
221 Ohmstead Street
Duluth, MN 55812
(218) 555-1546


OBJECTIVE:    A Position as Dietary Director


EXPERIENCE:   <u>Clinical Dietician</u>
              Riverside Nursing Care Facility    199_–present
              Duluth, MN

              Developed cost-effective nourishment program
              Established nutritional care standards for weight
              reduction, diabetic, and low-sodium diets

              <u>Clinical Dietician</u>
              City Hospital                       199_–9_
              Rochester, MN

              Prepared all menus
              Managed kitchen
              Assisted hospital administrator in planning and
              management of food services


EDUCATION:    <u>Dietary Intern</u>
              Burnsville Veterans Hospital        1990
              Burnsville, MN

              University of Minnesota
              M.S. in Nutrition                   199_

              B.S. in Food Service                199_

**EDUCATOR**

Hamilton Broadhurst
23 Sunset Lane
Milford, NH  03055
(603) 555-5134

## EMPLOYMENT OBJECTIVE

Seeking a position as an elementary school principal

## EDUCATION

Rivier College, M.Ed., 199_.  Major: Educational Administration
Thesis:  An Integrated Language Arts Curriculum
Keene State University, BE, 1985.  Major:  Elementary Education

## EXPERIENCE

199_ – present    Fourth Grade Teacher, Hollis Elementary School, Hollis, NH

* Initiated new program to help students with reading problems.
* Developed set of self-help exercises to teach students parts of speech.

1988–199_            Sixth Grade Teacher, Haid Elementary School, Nashua, NH

* Initiated math tutorial, with faster students helping those who needed extra help.
* Participated in Speak-Write experiment with teachers from three other schools.
* Member of Science Curriculum Committee. Helped revise science program for 5th and 6th grades.
* Chair of Language Arts Curriculum Committee.
* Evaluated and strengthened language arts curriculum in grades K-6.

## MEMBERSHIPS

National Education Association
New Hampshire Education Association
President-elect, Nashua Education Association

## PUBLICATIONS

"Let Students Teach Themselves the parts of Speech." *Elementary Education*, 72 (199_), 261–263.

"An Integrated Language Arts Curriculum." *Elementary Education*, 75 (199_), 49–56.

Credentials available from

University Placement Office
Hamilton Hall
Keene State University
Keene, NH  03072
(603)555-7800

**ENGINEER**

RUSSELL DEFIORI
1055 Amherst Street
Buffalo, NY 14214

(716) 555-1544

**OBJECTIVE**

Seeking employment as a mechanical engineer

**WORK EXPERIENCE**

1988 to present, Mechanical Engineer
Buffalo Manufacturing Company, Buffalo, NY

Responsible for machine and system design, production scheduling and quality control

Designed and installed electronically controlled bulk distribution system

Redesigned production equipment to create more efficient work flow and a higher quality end product

Produced feasibility study and cost estimate of 50,000 square foot warehouse

1986–1988  Quality Control Supervisor
Buffalo Manufacturing Company

Designed and supervised all product tests

**EDUCATION**

State University of New York at Albany — B.S. in mechanical engineering 1986

**MEMBERSHIPS**

American Society of Mechanical Engineers

REFERENCES AVAILABLE UPON REQUEST

INSURANCE

CARRIE BOROWICZ
2314 Larchmont Drive
Erie, PA 16509

(814) 555-2887

| | |
|---|---|
| **OBJECTIVE** | To apply extensive experience toward a position in insurance administration |
| **EXPERIENCE**<br>1992–present | **Claims Adjuster**<br>Fidelity Insurance Co., Carlisle, PA<br>Responsible for casualty insurance<br>Experienced in property evaluation |
| 1989–1992 | **Underwriter**<br>Hartford Insurance Co., Harrisburg, PA<br>Employed as clerk, promoted to underwriter after ten months<br>Followed underwriting guidelines to rate commercial insurance<br>Specialized in property and liability insurance |
| **EDUCATION**<br>1989 | A.A. degree in liberal arts<br>Lancaster County Community College<br>Lancaster, PA<br><br>Underwriters Board courses in casualty and general insurance |
| **MEMBERSHIPS** | Professional Underwriters of Pennsylvania |
| **REFERENCES** | Available upon request |

## MAINTENANCE SUPERVISOR

DAVI BHATT
332 West Side Drive
Kansas City, MO 64118
(816) 555-6621

**OBJECTIVE**

A position as Maintenance Supervisor in an Industrial Setting

**QUALIFICATIONS**

Fourteen years of experience in maintenance supervision. Master electrician. Skilled in carpentry, painting, and mechanical work.

**EXPERIENCE**

Maintenance Director
Brookhaven Nursing Home, Kansas City, MO      1991—present
- Responsible for 24 person staff that included housekeeping
  and maintenance personnel

Maintenance Manager
Central States Bag Company, St. Louis, MO     1988—91
- Supervised work of 15 mechanics and laborers
- Repaired all production equipment
- Supervised all routine maintenance

Night Shift Supervisor
Keppler & Jones, St. Louis, MO                1984—88
- Supervised night shift maintenance crew
- Responsible for janitorial crew and preventive maintenance

Electrician
Kepler & Jones                                1982—84
- Responsible for electrical maintenance and repair

**EDUCATION**

Graduate of U.S. Army Engineering School
Fort Belvoir, VA, 1981

Certificate in Stationary Engineering, Springfield Technical
Institute, 1982

**MEDICAL TECHNOLOGIST**

OLIVER FARNSWORTH
821 South Robertson Street
Chapel Hill, NC 27516

(919) 555-4331

**OBJECTIVE**      A position as director of technology in a small hospital

**EXPERIENCE**

199_–present      Supervisor of Technological Services
Greensboro Community Hospital, Greensboro, NC
- Directed work of two technicians
- Conducted all routine hospital tests of blood, skin, other tissues, cultures, and body fluids

1987–199_      Medical Technologist
Raleigh General Hospital, Raleigh, NC
- Conducted various tests
- Specialized in blood studies, primarily blood counts and blood cholesterol level

1983–1987      Medical Technologist
Willoughby Laboratories, Durham, NC
- Collected samples and ran routine tests

**EDUCATION**

1991      M.S. degree in Medical Technology
University of North Carolina

1983      B.S. degree in Medical Technology
University of North Carolina

Certified since 1983 by the North Carolina Registry of Medical Technologists

# PERSONNEL DIRECTOR

FRANCINE KAHN
135 Broad Street
Salem, MA 01970
(617) 555-7883

## OBJECTIVE

A position as Director of Personnel

## QUALIFICATIONS

Twelve years of highly successful experience in personnel work, including benefits administration, supervision, personnel development, recruitment, and training

### Benefits Administration
- Administered insurance benefits, including health, life, and short- and long-term disability
- Administered Worker's Compensation
- Administered Affirmative Action Program

### Personnel Development
- Helped design a program for personnel development
- Trained all new employees in a program designed to enhance individual esteem and present a favorable corporate image
- Trained office personnel in company policies and procedures

### Supervision
- Responsible for overall management of office personnel
- Directed activities of personnel department

### Recruitment
- Recruited, interviewed, and hired new office employees
- Wrote and evaluated job descriptions

## WORK HISTORY

**Director of Personnel**
Business Systems, Inc., Boston, MA          1988—present
**Personnel Assistant**
Webley Packaging, Newton, MA               1984—1988

## EDUCATION

A.S., Secretarial Science, Quincy Junior College, 1984

# RESTAURATEUR

Gregory Fleming
723 State Street
Portland, OR 97207

(503) 555-9887

## EXPERIENCE

**Manager: Swan's Way Restaurant, Eugene, OR** 1991–present
- Reestablished restaurant's reputation for fine cuisine
- Supervised all operations, including purchases, menus, and personnel
- Increased profits an average of 13% per year under my management

**Food and Beverage Manager, Mirabeau Hotel, Monmouth, OR** 1989–1991
- Supervised 40 employees in the preparation and serving of over 1200 quality meals per day
- Responsible for banquets and special events

**Chef, Brandenburg Restaurant, Indianapolis, IN** 1984–1989
- Hired as assistant chef; promoted to chef after six months
- Restaurant was listed as one of Indianapolis's best during my last two years as chef

**Cafeteria Manager, The Defiance College, Defiance, OH** 1982–1984
- Managed college cafeteria
- Planned and scheduled menus
- Hired and trained personnel
- Purchased all supplies

**First Cook, U.S. Army**                                     1979–1982

## EDUCATION

Oregon State University                     1978–1979
Corvallis, OR

U.S. Army Cooks & Bakers School                  1979
Four month course, Ft. Lee, VA

**Working knowledge of French and German**

OLETTA POND
21 Northwest 11th Court
Ft. Lauderdale, FL 33311
(305) 555-3477

## OBJECTIVE

Seeking a position as Department Manager in Public Supermarket

## EXPERIENCE

Little General Store, Hollywood, FL, 1990-present

* Took over "problem" store; within 4 months reduced employee turnover by 50%
* Brought inventory under control within 2 months
* Increased sales by an average of 15% a year
* Won award for outstanding store in region five times in two years
* Increased store visibility to public by participating in charity fund-raisers

Seven Eleven Store, Deerfield Beach, FL, 1987-90

* Began as clerk; was promoted to assistant manager within 2 months; was made manager 5 months later
* Implemented new display techniques
* Reorganized work schedules to cut down overtime
* Was consistently among top three stores in the region in sales increases

## EDUCATION

Attended Dade County Community College, Miami, FL, 1986-87

## ACTIVITIES

Florida State Special Olympics Committee
Member, South Florida Business Women's Association
Member, Friends of the Everglades

## REFERENCES

Available upon request

**SALES**

JANE AKALAITIS
87 Pleasant Street
Concord, NH 03301

603-555-1676

**OBJECTIVE**     To obtain a challenging position in marketing or sales

**EDUCATION**     Candidate for A.S. degree in Marketing
Hesser College, Manchester, NH 199_

**Courses in Retailing**

Salesmanship
Sales Management
Sales Psychology
Market Research
Marketing Seminar

**EXPERIENCE**     **Cashier**
Summers          First National Grocery Store, Concord, NH
199–199_

- Stocked shelves
- Served as cashier
- Substitute front-end supervisor

Oct.–present     **Sales Associate**
199_             Michaud's Clothing Store, Manchester, NH
(part-time)

- Served customers
- Arranged displays
- Ordered merchandise for women's department

**MEMBERSHIPS**     Vice President, Sales Club
Member Debate Team

**REFERENCES**     Placement Office
Hesser College
346 Elm Street
Manchester, NH 03103
(603) 555-3013

**TECHNICAL WRITER**

MORRIS KRESSLER
443 Evergreen Drive
Johnson City, TN 37614
615 555-2234

**OBJECTIVE**

Seeking a position in technical writing or editing

**EXPERIENCE**

1991—present        Alpha Engineering Company, Chattanooga, TN
                    **Technical Writer**

* Prepare bulletins and copy for technical advertising
* Work with engineering staff in preparing proposals
* Prepare engineering reports for clients
* Write technical manuals and brochures
* Write technical bulletins and specifications sheets

1987—1991          Electronics Magazine, Medford, MA
                   **Staff Writer**

* Wrote and edited articles on electronics and electrical engineering
* Wrote a monthly Question and Answer Column dealing with electronics

**EDUCATION**

Siena College, Memphis, TN
B.S. in Electrical Engineering
with Minor in English, 1987

Assistant Editor of Student Paper

**REFERENCES**

Available upon request

# Appendix B
# Checklist for Job Seekers

## INITIAL PREPARATIONS

- Analyze the job notice or want ad to discover the stated and unstated job requirements.
- Analyze yourself to find out how well your qualifications meet the requirements of the job opening.
- Draw up an inventory of your qualifications.
- Include statements in your inventory to demonstrate each of your qualifications.

## THE RESUME

- Decide whether a chronological, functional, or combined resume would be best for you.
- Write a career objective that shows what kind of job you're looking for. Be sure that the statement of objective doesn't block you in and cut you off from some openings that you might want.
- Put down your post-secondary education. List your high school only if you do not have any training beyond high school. Include any short courses, seminars, or workshops that are relevant to your career.
- List your significant work experience in reverse chronological order for a chronological resume or in skill clusters for a functional or combined resume.
- Describe your work responsibilities in a series of phrases beginning with active verbs.
- List any special skills, activities, professional memberships, or other relevant data in an appropriately labeled section.
- Ask several people if you can use them as references. Ask people who have authoritative positions and who know something about your work habits.
- Type your resume or have someone type it on good quality paper. Choose a format that looks good and well-balanced on the paper.
- Be sure that your resume has all the qualities it needs to succeed:
    - ★ Attractive
    - ★ Readable
    - ★ Persuasive
    - ★ Concise
    - ★ Focused

## COVER LETTERS

- Analyze the situation to determine whether a direct pattern or a persuasive cover letter would best serve your purpose. Also, decide whether an invited or a prospecting cover letter would be appropriate.

- Learn something about the company to which you are applying so that you can tailor your cover letter for that particular opening.

- Write a cover letter that gains attention, demonstrates capability, and confidently asks for an interview.

- Write your cover letter in a natural style.

- Be sure that your letter is grammatically correct and that everything is spelled correctly.

- Let your letter enhance your resume by giving specific information about your qualifications for a specific job.

## THE INTERVIEW

- Mentally focus on your strengths so that you can develop a positive attitude.

- Go over the list of frequently asked interview questions in Chapter 6. Decide how you would respond to each question.

- Prepare a work history sheet to help you fill out an employment application.

- Get a reference sheet ready to take to the interview with you.

- Dress conservatively to present a favorable impression.

- Go to the interview confidently.

- Answer questions completely, honestly, and confidently.

## THE FOLLOW-UP LETTER

- Immediately after the interview, write to the person who interviewed you to thank him or her.

- Refer to something you learned about the organization from the interview and express a continued interest in the position.

# Glossary

**active verb**   A verb that shows action. These verbs can strengthen a resume and cover letter because they demonstrate what an applicant has already done.

**application form**   A form that is usually filled out before the employment interview. It asks for information about an individual's work history and education. Application forms need to be filled out neatly and completely.

**chronological resume**   A resume, also called a standard or conventional resume, that emphasizes a job seeker's work history. On this type of resume, the job seeker's experience is listed in reverse chronological order, starting with the most recent employment.

**combined resume**   A resume that combines the strengths of the chronological resume with those of the functional resume. As in the functional resume, it lists a series of skill clusters designed to demonstrate an applicant's ability to perform a particular job. In addition to the skill clusters, the combined resume has a chronological work history.

**corporate personality**   Just like individuals, companies have distinct personalities. Some companies are formal and rigid; others are more relaxed and informal. The corporate personality includes such things as manner of dress and relations between management and subordinates. Knowing something about the corporate personality can be a distinct advantage in preparing a resume and cover letter and in a job interview.

**cover letter**   A letter that accompanies the resume. A cover letter may be direct pattern and merely tell the employer that the writer wants to be considered for a position and that a resume is enclosed; or a cover letter can be persuasive and try to enhance the resume by adding information about the writer's qualifications for a position in a particular company.

**direct pattern cover letter**   A letter, accompanying the resume, that is brief and to the point. This letter says, "Here is my resume. I'm interested in the job opening that you advertised."

**employment counselor**   Someone who works at a governmental, private, or college placement office. An employment counselor helps job seekers find appropriate openings, write resumes and cover letters, and prepare for the employment interview.

**entry-level position**   A starting position within an organization or career. Typically, people with little experience in a particular career start at an entry-level position.

**focused resume**   A resume that emphasizes an applicant's qualifications for a particular career or job. A focused resume might be contrasted with a general resume, which gives the applicant's qualifications without regard to a specific area of employment.

**follow-up letter**   A letter written after some kind of initial contact has been made with an organization regarding a job opening. Follow-up letters may thank an employer for an interview or express an interest in being considered for future openings within an organization.

**format**   The way a resume is arranged on a page. There are many effective formats for resumes. An effective format is balanced and looks attractive on the page.

**functional resume**   A resume that emphasizes an individual's qualifications for a job by arranging an applicant's experience in skill clusters rather than in chronological order.

**general purpose resume**   A resume that can be used for more than one type of job.

**group interview**   An interview in which a group of people interview a job applicant.

**illegal question**   A question that may not legally be asked in an interview; for example, a question about ethnic background, religion, or marital status.

**interests**   An applicant's personal interests were once included on resumes. Most authorities now recommend that they be omitted.

**interviewer**   Someone who conducts an employment interview. An interviewer is typically someone in a company's personnel department or a manager. Sometimes interviewers from personnel departments will screen applicants before sending them to managers for a final interview.

**inventory of qualifications**   A list of an applicant's qualifications for a particular job. The inventory might include experience, education, and personal attributes. Such an inventory can be very helpful in preparing to draft a resume.

**invited application**   A resume and cover letter sent in response to a notification of a job opening such as a want ad or a notice to a placement agency.

**job requirements**   A list of the qualifications required for a particular job opening. For example, the job requirements for a secretary might include being able to type, answer the telephone, and file documents. A particular job might also require a secretary to have other skills such as shorthand or word processing.

**natural style**   Cover letters should avoid pompous, stilted writing, archaic phrases, and technical jargon. They should be written in a natural, conversational style.

**objective (career objective)**   One of the first sections of the resume. It tells the employer which job the applicant is interested in.

**personal attributes**   Personal qualities such as leadership, communication skill, or organizational ability. Employers look for evidence of these attributes in the resume, the cover letter, and the employment interview.

**personal data**   Personal information such as age, health, religion, ethnic background, and marital status. These things were once included in resumes. However, they may no longer be taken into account in deciding to whom to offer a job. For this reason, it is inappropriate to put then on a resume.

**personalized cover letter**   A cover letter that is focused toward a particular job opening. A personalized cover letter makes some direct references to the company where the job opening exists. It also enhances the resume by referring to the applicant's qualifications for a specific position, especially if those qualifications are not listed on the resume.

**persuasive cover letter**   A letter, accompanying the resume, whose purpose is to enhance the resume in such a way as to persuade the reader that the applicant has the qualifications required for a job.

**placement folder**   Many university placement offices keep folders for students or graduates who register with them. These folders contain letters of recommendation, transcripts, and other material that pertains to one's job qualifications. If a job applicant is registered with such a university placement office, the prospective employer needs only to contact the placement office rather than all of the applicant's references.

**placement office**   Most colleges and technical schools have a placement office to help their students and graduates find employment. Typically, placement offices bring students together with prospective employers. They usually also help the students with resumes and preparations for interviews.

**prospecting cover letter**   A cover letter, accompanying a resume, sent to an organization when the applicant doesn't know whether the company has a job opening. The advantage of a prospecting application is that there will be less competition for a position if it hasn't been advertised or announced in some official way.

**qualifications**   The capabilities, competencies, skills, etc., that show that an applicant can perform a particular job. Generally speaking, an applicant's main qualifications are experience and education.

**reference**   A person who knows something about an applicant's work habits and is willing to write about them. Former teachers and work supervisors are authoritative references. Most resumes make a statement about the availability of references.

**reference sheet**   A piece of paper prepared in advance of a job interview that contains the names, job titles, work addresses, and day-time telephone numbers of the people an applicant lists as references.

**resume**   A sheet that summarizes an individual's qualifications for a job.

**skill clusters**   Groups of activities that demonstrate particular qualifications for a job.

**"snow storm" letters**   A form cover letter sent out with a large number of resumes. "Snow storm" letters are usually less effective than individually written letters because they are not focused toward specific openings.

**standard resume**   Also known as a chronological resume. On this type of resume, work experience is listed in reverse chronological order.

**stress interview**   An interview in which the interviewer deliberately tries to make the person being interviewed feel uncomfortable. The purpose of such an interview is to see how well the applicant performs under pressure. Very few actual job interviews fall into this category, and it is not appropriate to use this type of interview unless the ability to work under pressure is necessary on the job.

**style**   The way a resume presents the qualifications of a job applicant.

**thank-you letter**   Letter written by a job applicant after an interview that thanks the prospective employer for the interview. This letter is both a courtesy and an opportunity for the applicant to reaffirm interest in the job and, if necessary, to add something about his or her qualifications that may have been omitted during the interview.

**volunteer work**   Work for which one is not paid, but at which a job applicant might learn special skills or have experiences that are relevant to a particular job opening. Volunteer work can be included on a resume, especially if an applicant has no actual experience in the area and the work is relevant to a position for which the applicant is applying.

**work history sheet**   A sheet prepared in advance of a job interview that provides all relevant information about an applicant's job history.

# Bibliography

**Asher, Donald.** *The Overnight Resume.* Berkeley, CA: Ten Speed Press, 1991.

**Bolles, Richard Nelson.** *What Color Is Your Parachute?* Berkeley, CA: Ten Speed Press, 1991.

**Byrne, John A.** "A Shot in the Dark." *Forbes* 22 April 1985: 136.

**Byrne, John A.** "The Dos and Don'ts of Writing a Resume." *Business Week* 6 October 1986: 102.

"Changing Faces . . . Changing Places." *Business Digest.* August 1988: 16–22+.

**Cohen, Steve and Paul de Oliveira.** "Resumes." *Getting To the Right Job.* New York: Workman, 1987: 123–145.

**Cole, Diane.** "Getting Your Name On Everyone's Lips." *Working Woman* August 1989: 68–70.

**DuMont, Raymond A. and John M. Lannon.** "The Job Application Letter." *Business Communications.* 2nd Ed. Boston: Little Brown, 1987: 485–492.

**Eflein, Cindy.** "Job Hunting Mistakes, Goofs and Blunders." *Careers Unlimited* April 1988: 10–12.

**Eyler, David R.** *Resumes That Mean Business.* New York: Random House, 1990.

**Fischer, Arlene.** "How To Find A Job You Love." *Redbook* April 1991: 110–111+.

**Fry, Ronald W.** *Your First Resume.* Hawthorne, NJ: Career Press, 1989.

**Guffey, Mary Ellen.** *Essentials of Business Communication.* Boston: PWS-Kent, 1988: 266.

**Harcourt, Jules, et al.** "Teaching Resume Content: Hiring Officials' Preference Versus College Recruiters' Preference." *Business Education Forum* April 1991: 13–17.

**Harragan, Betty Lehan.** "Writing the Right Cover Letter." *Mademoiselle* October 1984: 242–244.

"Job Hunting in the Work Jungle." *Working Women* April 1987: 100–101.

**Johnston, R. Ernest.** "Resumes: Let Common Sense Guide You." *Maine Sunday Telegram* 14 August 1988: 6H.

**Kennedy, Marilyn Moats.** "What They Don't Tell You About Why You Didn't Get the Job." *Glamour* May 1991: 117.

**Kent, George E.** *How To Get Hired Today!* Lincolnwood, IL: VGM Career Horizons, 1991.

**King, Pamela.** "Using Contacts To Get Jobs." *Psychology Today* 14 June 1989: 14.

**Krannich, Ronald L.** *High Impact Resumes and Letters.* Manassas, VA: Impact Publications, 1988.

**Lewis, Adele Beatrice.** *How To Write Better Resumes.* 3rd Ed. New York: Barron's Educational Series, 1989.

**Moreau, Daniel.** "Write A Resume That Works." *Changing Times* June 1990: 91.

**Morino, Kim.** *The College Student's Resume Guide.* Santa Barbara, CA: Tangerine Press, 1989.

**Nivens, Beatryce.** "How To Write A Winning Resume." *Essence* November 1987: 114.

**Parker, Yana.** *The Damn Good Resume Guide.* Berkeley, CA: Ten Speed Press, 1986.

**Payne, Richard A.** *How To Get A Better Job Quicker.* 3rd Ed. New York: Taplinger Publishing Co., 1987.

**Plawin, Paul.** "Job-Hunting Blunders You Don't Want To Make." *Changing Times* December 1988: 67+.

**Plawin, Paul.** "Looking For That First Job." *Changing Times* August 1987: 78.

**Saralegui, Maite.** "Writing A Right-On Resume." *Mademoiselle* 6 September 1984: 295–296.

**Schmidt, Peggy J.** *The 90-Minute Resume.* Princeton, NJ: Peterson's Guide, 1990.

**Silver, Marc.** "Selling the Perfect You." *U.S. News and World Report* 2 February 1990: 70–72.

**Wilkinson, C.W. et al.** "Evaluating Yourself and Potential Employers." *Communicating Through Letters and Reports.* 8th Ed. Homewood, IL: Richard D. Irwin, 1983: 278–313.

# Software Applications

| Filename | Chapter | Topic | Description |
|---|---|---|---|
| GUIDE1 | 1 | Getting Started | This application helps you learn how to identify specific requirements for various positions and to translate such requirements from job advertisements. The application provides practice in determining job requirements by looking at stated requirements and analyzing the position to discover the unstated requirements and create itemized lists. |
| GUIDE2 | 1 | Qualifications Inventory | This application leads you through the process of drawing up an inventory of your qualifications and beginning the process of presenting evidence of those qualifications. After completing this step, you are ready to prepare your resume elements. |
| GUIDE3 | 2 | Resume Elements | This application and the next both focus on the content of your resume. These two applications will help you organize concise, focused, and persuasive information for the resumes that you prepare. This application helps you ensure that each element on your resume reveals one of your qualifications. In this application, you will be provided with practice in setting up and phrasing your resume in such a way as to emphasize your qualifications for a position you are interested in. |
| GUIDE4 | 2 | Building from Notecards | This application will help you create a database of notecards that you can use to prepare resumes and cover and follow-up letters. |
| GUIDE5 | 3 | Format | This application gives you help in producing attractive, easy-to-read resumes based on content you created for yourself in previous activities. In this application you explore the advantages and disadvantages of presenting information in three types of formats—*functional, chronological,* and *combination.* |
| GUIDE6 | 4 | Cover Letters | This application explores the different types of cover letters. In this application you use template samples of *direct pattern* and *persuasive* cover letters that you can edit and adapt for your own use. |
| GUIDE7 | 7 | Follow-Up Letters | This application presents several types and purposes of follow-up letters that you must analyze. You are then given the opportunity to practice writing each type, with samples available to edit and adapt for your own purposes. |

# (IBM) Documentation for INTENTIONAL EDUCATIONS' WRITING SYSTEM SOFTWARE

# The Intentional Writing System

## NECESSARY HARDWARE

The program disk runs on the IBM PC, XT, or AT and many IBM compatibles with at least one disk drive and a minumum of 256 K of available RAM. The program runs under DOS 3.0 or later.

A printer is optional. The printers supported by the program are:

all Epson printers and compatibles
all IBM/ProPrinter printers and compatibles
HP Laser Jet and all compatibles

Your work is saved on a separate data disk (as files with the extension .WRI). Use an MS-DOS formatted disk to store your work or save your work to your hard drive.

## HARD DRIVE INSTALLATION

If you have a hard drive you may install the program on it and run the program from there, while saving your work on floppies. Boot your machine the way you would normally. After the machine has booted, put the program disk into your floppy drive but do not change drives. Type:

| | |
|---|---|
| CD \ ⟨Enter⟩ | (root directory) |
| MD WRISYST ⟨Enter⟩ | (make subdirectory for program) |
| CD WRISYST ⟨Enter⟩ | (change to that directory) |
| COPY A:*.* ⟨Enter⟩ | (copy all files from A:\) |
| MD GUIDES ⟨Enter⟩ | (make subdirectory for .gui files) |
| CD \WRISYST\GUIDES ⟨Enter⟩ | (change to that directory) |
| COPY A:\GUIDES\*.* ⟨Enter⟩ | (copy all files from A:\GUIDES subdirectory) |

To start the program, change directories to WRISYST and type GO at the prompt. When the program opens the default data drive is C, so if you want to save your work to a floppy, you must use Data Drive from the Help Menu (see below) before opening a file.

## FLOPPY DRIVE USE

If your machine has two floppy drives, use the a: drive for the program disk, and the b: drive for your data disk. From the A⟩ prompt type GO.

## QUICK GUIDE FOR USING THE PROGRAM

### HOW TO BEGIN

All the features of the program appear in the menu bar across the top of the screen. Notice the prompt area at the bottom of the screen. It always shows you how to use the program.

When the menu bar first appears, if the File Menu is automatically pulled down, the New function is highlighted. Select New from the File Menu by pressing ⟨Enter⟩ to create a file in which you will do your writing. The program selects a drive on which to save your work. To change where the program saves your work, select Data Drive from the Help Menu (see below).

Once you have opened a file, you can use the Guide Menu to select lessons and exercises. The Practice Menu contains special files you can insert into your work. The Notes Menu contains a database of notecards you can use for yor work.

The other pull-down menus (Help, File, Edit, and Display) provide normal word-processing options and functions that affect what you enter in your file.

Shortcut keys are listed next to some menu options. You can type the shortcut keys without pulling down a menu. When a menu option is inactive, it is grayed out on the menu. (For instance, all options on the Guide, Practice, and Notes Menus are inactive if you do not have a file open.)

## CHANGING GUIDE LESSONS

You can change lessons at any time by simply selecting another lesson from the Guide Menu. To return to a lesson, just select it again. Within a session, a lesson will be reopened at the place where you left it. You can also use ⟨ESC⟩ to close a lesson in order to make the full screen available for your writing and then rechoose it to continue.

## HELP MENU

**About Program** gives information about the publisher and developer of the program.

**Help** (⟨F1⟩) is available from any part of the word processing program. When you access a Help Screen, you are really looking at one page in the Help Book. Some pages in the Help Book give general information; others tell about the function that is presently active. Most of the information in this User's Reference is in the Help Book. Use ← and → to move back and forth in the Help Book.

**Help Commands**

| | |
|---|---|
| ⟨F1⟩ | display Help for the current function |
| ⟨ESC⟩ | exit Help |
| ⟨ARROWS⟩ | move forward or backward through Help |
| ⟨PgUp/PgDn⟩ | move forward or backward through Help |
| ⟨HOME⟩ | go to Page 1 of Help |
| ⟨END⟩ | go to the last page of Help |

**Data Drive** allows you to change where the program will look for the data disk, referred to as the "default" data drive. Ordinarily this will be drive C. It displays the current drive and prompts you to enter the letter of the drive where you want your work saved. You cannot change drives while a file is open.

## FILE MENU

The File Menu enables you to end your work in a file, as well as do other things such as printing and saving your files.

**New File** begins a new file. A file must be open in order to do any work in the writer. If you wish to open a new file for a different exercise, close the open file and then select New. Enter a filename (up to 8 characters). Then begin work.

**Open File** (⟨F4⟩) opens any file that was created with this software and saved on your data disk. Select Open File (when no file is open), highlight a filename from the list that appears, and press ⟨Enter⟩.

(Note: If the file you want is not displayed, it may have been saved to a different drive or on another disk. You can ⟨ESC⟩ back to the menus and use Data Drive to change the default data drive and check. See Data Drive, above.) If you have created any new files for other exercises, use Open File to open them.

**Close File** closes a file when you want to stop working on it. If you have not saved your most recent work, a prompt will ask you if you want to save the file before you close it. If you press N, you close your file without saving it. If you press Y, you are asked whether you want to save the file with the current name. If you answer N you are prompted to supply another name, under which the file will be saved.

**Insert File** merges files. Locate the cursor where the file is to be inserted, select Insert File, and in the prompt area enter the name of the file you want to insert. Any file made with this program and saved on the same data disk you are currently using may be inserted into any file on which you are currently working.

**Save File** (⟨F3⟩) saves an open file in its present version and allows you to continue working on it. This command is used only while you have a file open. (To stop working, use Close File.) A prompt will appear asking you to confirm saving with the same file name. If you press Y for Yes the present version copies over the older version.

To save changes you have made to a file without replacing the original file, choose Save File; then when you are asked if you want to use the same name, press N for No, and type in a new name for the file into the prompt area; then press ⟨Enter⟩.

A warning message appears when there is not enough room on your data disk to save the file. If this happens, remove the data disk that is in the drive, insert another formatted data disk; then save your work to that disk.

**Save as ASCII** saves a copy of the open file in ASCII format. This command is used only while you have a file open. A prompt will appear asking if you want to save with the same file name. If you press N, you will be prompted to enter a new name for the file.

When a file is saved as an ASCII file the program cannot open it. The file is stripped of all special formatting. This is useful if you want to give a copy of your work on disk to someone (like your teacher) who uses a different word processing program that can open ASCII files. The ASCII files have a filename extension of .ASC.

**Print File** (⟨F5⟩) prints the file you are working on. The program's printing options are preset as shown in the right-hand column below. They may be changed, within the limits in parentheses in the middle column. The program does not allow you to use numbers outside those limits. Options remain as set until you change them again or until you reload the program. (They revert to the default values when you quit the program.)

| Title | FILENAME | |
|---|---|---|
| Left Margin | (1–65) | 7 |
| Right Margin | (10–80) | 75 |
| Line Spacing | (1–3) | 1 |
| Top Line | (1–60) | 7 |
| Bottom Line | (7–90) | 60 |
| Paper Length | (6–90) | 66 |
| Stop between Pages | (Y or N) | N |
| Page Numbering | (Y or N) | Y |
| Start at Page | | 1 |
| Stop after Page | | 99 |

Change "Stop between Pages" to Y for Yes if you intend to feed paper by hand. If the line spacing does not come out as you expected, check your printer manual for setup routines.

**Copy File** duplicates a file that you choose from your data disk and puts the duplicate on the same data disk. You can use this feature only when no file is open. To copy a file, select the file and type in the new filename for the copy; then press ⟨Enter⟩.

**Rename File** enables you to give a new name to any file on your data disk. You can use this feature only when no file is open. To rename a file, select the file and type in the new filename; then press ⟨Enter⟩.

**Erase File** deletes files made with this program. Use Erase File to get rid of files you no longer want and to free up space on your data disk. You can use this feature only when no file is open.

**Quit** closes the file you have open and quits the program. If you have not saved your most recent work, a prompt will ask you if you want to save it before you close the file.

## EDIT MENU

**Undo** (⟨F9⟩) cancels the last Move, Copy, or Delete Text command. (You cannot undo other commands.) You can use the Undo function only immediately after you've moved, copied, or deleted text and before pressing any other keys.

**Copy Text** (⟨F7⟩) duplicates a part of your document. Select Copy Text, then follow the instructions in the prompt area to highlight the text to copy; then move the cursor to the place to insert the copy and press ⟨Enter⟩. A copy of the text will appear in the new palce.

**Move Text** (⟨F8⟩) allows you to mark a part of your document and move it to another place in your document. Select Move Text, then follow the instructins in the prompt area to highlight the text to move; then move the cursor to the new location and press ⟨Enter⟩. The highlighted text will be moved from the old location to the new.

**Delete Text** (⟨F6⟩) allows you to mark a part of your document and erase it. Select Delete Text, then follow the instruction in the prompt area to highlight the text you want to delete and press ⟨Enter⟩.

**Overstrike** (⟨INS⟩) allows you to switch between Insert and Overstrike text entry mode. The bottom right corner of the screen indicates which text entry mode is active.

## FIND MENU

**Find** enables you to instruct the program to locate every occurrence of a "string" of characters. (A "string" is any combination of letters, numbers, symbols, and spaces that you enter. It can be one letter, part of a word, or several words, up to the limit of 25 characters.) Choose Find from the Find Menu, then in the prompt area type in characters and spaces, exactly the way you want them found; then press ⟨Enter⟩. Find starts at the cursor, loops through the end of the file and back to the cursor position until every instance of the string is found. Press ⟨ESC⟩ to cancel Find.

**Replace** replaces strings of characters. For example, if you had typed "Jonson" instead of "Johnson," you could easily correct it everywhere it occurs. Choose Replace from the Find Menu, then type in the characters and spaces that you want to replace in the prompt area, then press ⟨Enter⟩. Then type exactly what you want used instead and press ⟨Enter⟩. (Although the Find function ignores upper and lower case, the replacement will use the upper and lower case characters exactly as you specify). Each time the string is found, the program asks if you want to replace it. Strings for replacement may be up to 25 characters long. ⟨ESC⟩ stops the Replace command but leaves all the changes already made.

## DISPLAY MENU

Functions on the Display Menu determine how your work will appear in print only. By choosing Preview Print (see below) you can see on screen how these options will appear when you print your work.

**Bold** (Ctrl-B) Use this command immediately before and immediately after the characters you want to appear in boldface. On the screen, B⟩ marks the beginning of boldface and ⟨B marks the end.

**Underline** (Ctrl-U) Use this command immediately before and immediately after characters you want underlined. On the screen, U⟩ marks the beginning of underlining and ⟨U marks the end.

**Quote** (Ctrl-Q) Use this command immediately before and immediately after direct quotations. On the screen, Q⟩ marks the beginning of the quote and ⟨Q marks the end.

**Center** (Cntrl-C) Select the Center command to mark the beginning of the text you want centered. On the screen, C⟩ marks the beginning of centering. Everything will be centered until the next carriage return. (If text to center is longer than one line, all lines preceding the carriage return will be centered.)

**New Page** (Ctrl-N) starts a new page. The symbol N⟩ is displayed, and the cursor moves to the next line.

**Left Margin** (Ctrl-L) Each time you give this command, the left margin is indented five spaces. (Use this command and twice to indent your text ten spaces, etc.) The increased left margin remains in effect until the program encounters a carriage return in your text. To see how your work will appear choose Preview Print.

**Right Margin** (Ctrl-R) indents the right margin five spaces for each time you press it. (Use this command twice to indent the right side of your text ten spaces, etc.) The increased right margin remains in effect until the program encounters a carriage return. To see how your work will appear choose Preview Print.

**Line Spacing** (Ctrl-S) sets line spacing (1⟩, 2⟩, or 3⟩). Select Line Spacing from the Display Menu, then type 1 for single spacing, 2 for double spacing, or 3 for triple spacing. The spacing remains as set until you change it. This command is useful when you want to change the line spacing for part of a document. To see how your work will appear choose Preview Print.

**Page & Line Count** tells you, in the prompt area, the location of the cursor in your text.

**Preview Print** displays a facsimile of a printed page on the left side of the screen with your text on the right. It shows the effects of any Display Menu commands you have used on your document—centering, spacing, etc. ⟨ARROWS⟩ move the cursor in the facsimile. Cancel Preview Print by pressing ⟨ESC⟩ to resume editing the file with the cursor at that location. Preview Print does not display on a computer without a graphics card.

## GUIDE MENU

To do the exercises, choose one listed under the Guide Menu.

Whenever you choose an exercise, the computer screen splits horizontally, with the exercise that you chose appearing in the bottom part of the screen. Your working area (text entry area) remains at the top. You can still write in the text area and use the pull-down menus.

When the exercise appears, the prompt area displays the commands you need to page through it. Each lesson contains a number of "pages" of information. Use ⟨Ctrl-G⟩ to go forward and ⟨Ctrl-T⟩ to go backward through the lesson, a page at a time. The prompt area tells you where you are in the lesson. (For example, "Page 3 of 9.") You can still use ⟨F2⟩ to pull down the menus and ⟨F1⟩ to get online Help about using the word processing functions.

When an exercise is open, you can switch back to the full screen to write. Pressing ⟨ESC⟩ or selecting Exit Guide from the Guide Menu closes the guidance window at the bottom of the screen. When you reselect that exercise from the Guide Menu, the program remembers where you were and picks up right where you left off. (When you Quit the program, it forgets, but it is easy to page down to where you want to be in any exercise whenever you reboot the program and return to an exercise.)

**Exit Guide**, the last item on the Guide Menu, closes the bottom (exercise) window. Use Exit Guide when you have finished with an exercise, or to switch back to the full screen for writing. To switch back and forth between two exercises when you have one displayed already, just select the other exercise from the menu. It will appear in the exercise window at the bottom of the screen. When you reselect the previous exercise, it will pick up just where you left off.

## PRACTICE MENU

Making a selection from the Practice Menu places text in the open file so you can use the word processor to edit it. Selections from this menu can be reused repeatedly. Any changes that you make in your file do not change the text items on this menu.

## NOTE MENU

The Note Menu opens a database file of "records." Prompts for using the file appear when it is active. You may not type in your file while the Note options are in use.

**View** opens the file for browsing. If a record is too large to fit in the area at the bottom of the screen, use the Up and Down ⟨ARROWS⟩ to scroll the record. To move from one record to the next use the ⟨PgUp⟩ and ⟨PgDn⟩ keys. Pressing ⟨ESC⟩ closes the file.

**Edit** opens the database file with your cursor in it to enable you to edit records. Use the ⟨ARROWS⟩ to move the cursor in the record. Whatever you type will be entered at the cursor. The total amount allowed in each file is as follows:

paraphrase or quotation—710 characters
source—120 characters
note—250 characters

The ⟨INS⟩ key toggles between insert and overstrike mode. The ⟨Delete⟩ and ⟨backspace⟩ keys enable you to erase. To move from one record to the next use the ⟨PgUp⟩ and ⟨PgDn⟩ keys. Pressing ⟨ESC⟩ closes the file

**Find** lets you select specific records by finding those that have a common element that you ask the program to look for. Choose Find from the Note Menu, then press ⟨Enter⟩. Type into the appropriate field the characters that you want the program to search for. Press ⟨Ctrl-X⟩ when you want to begin the search. Continue to follow the on-screen prompting to answer the whether to begin or ⟨ESC⟩ to cancel the search.

Find will make active only those records that contain characters to match what you typed in. When the search is completed, the status line at the bottom of the screen will tell you how many records are active. When Find is used again, it will search through only the active records. With each new search, you are working with successively smaller and smaller subsets of the database file, until you press ⟨Ctrl-A⟩ to return to all records for a brand new search. To make all the records active, press ⟨Ctrl-A⟩.

**Copy** enables you to mark a part of a record and put it into your open file, where you may use the word processor to edit it. Use View or Find from the Note Menu to choose the record from which you want to copy. Then select Copy from the Note Menu. The cursor will appear in the record. Follow the instructions in the prompt area to highlight what you want to copy then press ⟨Enter⟩. The cursor will then appear in your writing file. Move it to the place wher you want to insert the copy and press ⟨Enter⟩.

## SPECIAL KEYS

Listed below are special function keys available in the word processing program.

| | |
|---|---|
| ⟨F1⟩ | Help |
| ⟨F2⟩ | Menu |
| ⟨F3⟩ | Save File |
| ⟨F4⟩ | Open File |
| ⟨F5⟩ | Print File |
| ⟨F6⟩ | Delete Text |
| ⟨F7⟩ | Copy Text |
| ⟨F8⟩ | Move Text |
| ⟨F9⟩ | Undo |
| ⟨ESC⟩ | cancel a command, back out of a screen |
| ⟨ARROWS⟩ | move the cursor |
| ⟨BACKSPACE⟩ | erase backward (to the left of the cursor) |
| ⟨DEL⟩ | erase forward (erase the cursor character) |
| ⟨INS⟩ | change between INSERT and OVERSTRIKE |

Menus show other short cut keys (such as simultaneous use of the Control and U keys to mark text to underline). When you see ⟨Ctrl-⟩ followed by a letter, hold down the Control key while you press the letter key. The ∧ symbol represents ⟨Ctrl⟩ on the pull-down menus.

# Index

requirements of interviewer, 74
stress interview, 81–82
Job placement agencies, 8–9
Job requirements, 2
Job seeker checklist, 109–10

# M

Memberships, 31
Model resumes, 94–108

# N

Natural style, 67

# O

Oliveira, Paul de, 32

# P

Personal attributes, 12
Personal data, 33
Personalized cover letter, 55–56
Persuasive cover letter, 53–57
Persuasiveness in resume, 19
Placement offices, 8–9
*Portland Press Herald*, 62
Prospecting cover letter, 57–60

# Q

Qualifications, 1
    demonstrating, 13–14
    inventory of, 12

# R

Readability in resume, 19
References, 32–33
Reference sheet, 78
Resume
    activities, honors, awards, memberships, and skills, 31
    characteristics of winning resume, 17
        attractiveness, 18
        conciseness, 19
        focus, 19–20

persuasiveness, 19
readability, 19
chronological, 50
combined, 28, 44, 47
copies of, 33
education section, 26–27
experience section, 28–30
format and length of, 33
functional, 21, 24, 40, 44
heading for, 24
interests, 31–32
models of, 94–108
objective of, 24–25
personal data, 33
preparing to write, 1–14
references, 32
revised, 47
updated, 36, 38
Revised resume, 47

# S

Self-confidence, 71–73
Skill clusters, 21
Skills, 31
"Snow storm" letters, 61
Software applications, 115
Stress interview, 81–82

# T

Thank-you letter, 87
*The Reader's Guide*, 62, 75

# U

Updated resume, 36, 38

# V

Volunteer work, 12

# W

Work experience, 12
Work history sheet, 78
Writing style, 64, 67–68